quilty

12 Easy Patchwork Quilts
& Quilting Advice

Mary Fons &
Team Quilty

Fons&Porter

CINCINNATI, OH

contents

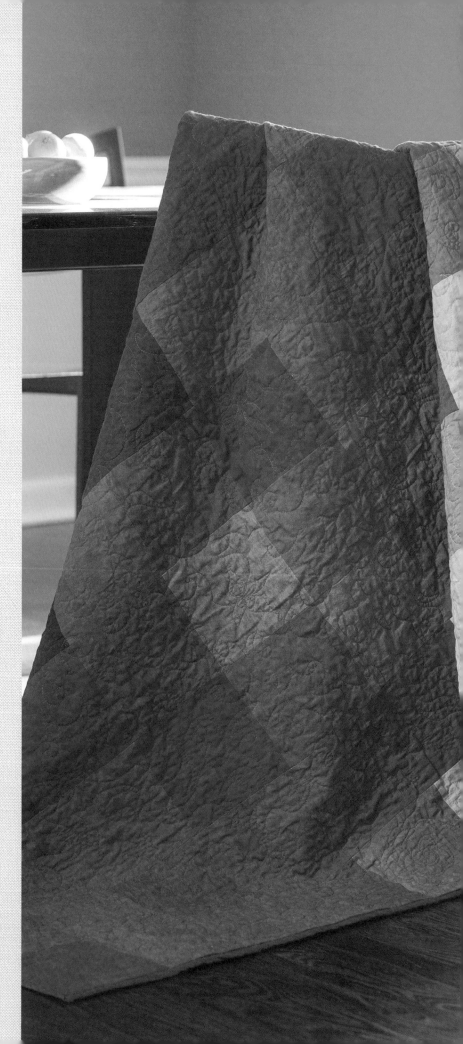

Hey *Quilty*,

One Sunday afternoon, I made a run to the grocery store without my kids (Hubby had them at home cleaning out the camping supplies for the summer). I love going to the grocery store, especially by myself. I get to take my time, read all the labels, and no one asks me repeatedly, "Can we get that, can we get that?! Can we? Can we?" I get to discover new things—and I discovered you!

First, I filled my cart with the items on my list. Then I went over to the magazines, straight to the craft section. I've been scrapbooking and crafting for years—I am a newbie quilter. My obsession began in October. I made a Christmas quilt. I was sure it would be totally wonky, but I figured if it was for Christmas, I would only have to take it out once a year. Well, it stayed on my couch until May. It was way too much work for me to fold that puppy up and pack it away for ten months. The addiction begins.

Since finishing that quilt in December, I've taken a few classes, upgraded my sewing machine, and have started to sell some of my smaller sewing projects to support my fat quarter addiction. My second quilt was a T-shirt quilt for my oldest daughter. That little tip about using interfacing would have been GREAT to know about two months ago! My next investment before I make my next T-shirt quilt will be a large ruled square for sure. I read pages 43 and 44 [Spring/Summer 2012] repeatedly saying "Man, why didn't I do that?!"

Finding a quilting magazine, especially for a newbie, is tough. There are so many magazines out there, but until YOU, there wasn't a one that I connected with. I love *Quilty*. You should see it. It's been mine for about a month now and it looks like it's a year old. It is well-loved. First, the Moda ad, then the Quilty chair… And Spooly! I love me some Spooly! I'm hooked. One-third of the way through I had a tough choice to make: keep reading or visit your website. (I should have been cooking dinner, but really, do they need to eat again? I feed them EVERY DAY!) I read one more page and then proceeded to watch no less than four videos before my natives were beyond restless and threatened to touch the things in my kitchen.

Hey, *Quilty*, I love you and I'm going to need your next issue sooner rather than later. So stop reading this letter and get back to work.

The Newbie Who Needs Ya,
Carmen Hernandez
Sent from my iPad

Carmen can come over for Quilty cake anytime. (Celebrating 200th *Quilty* episode, 2014.)

INTRODUCTION

Now Is the Best Time to Make a Quilt

BY MARIANNE FONS

A COMMON NOTION is that "everything was better in the old days." More than once when chatting with a non-quilter, if I reveal we work our patchwork magic mostly by machine these days, my listener's eyes become misty. He, or she—usually a person who has not held a needle or wound a bobbin, ever—becomes nostalgic. Spoken or not, the sentiment "They just don't make 'em like they used to" is in the air.

Most quilty people dedicate more time to playing with fabric and actually making quilts than studying the history of quiltmaking. (Of this, I can only approve: buy fabric! It keeps our industry thriving!) However, we who ply the needle might also operate under the mistaken notion that quilters of yesteryear (the Colonists maybe?) somehow had it better than we do, especially when we look at an antique Mariner's Compass so fabulous it seems untouched by human hands.

The truth is, right now is probably the best time in American history to be making quilts. To prove my point, let me take you on a little journey back in time.

History Worth Knowing

Colonial days were a terrible time to quilt, unless you were rich. Beautiful, exotic chintzes, on trend then in London and Paris, were the rage among fashionistas of the New World, too. Everyone (men and women, but only the wealthy ones) dressed in these gorgeous fabrics.

Glazed chintz was *de rigueur* for window drapes and bed curtains as well. Printed in India, such fabrics were imported to England, then sent across the pond to the Americas, the price jacked up by every pair of hands that touched them en route. Even the rich had to cut them apart to justify the cost; clever (wealthy) needlewomen separated the birds-of-paradise, the palm trees, and the cornucopias from the whole cloth, appliquéing these motifs to cheaper, plain fabric to cover their beds and grace the windows of their homes. Only ladies of leisure married to influential men had quilts.

Once America belonged to the Americans, the next big revolution on our shores was the Industrial Revolution. Cotton growers in southern states supplied the raw material for textile mills in the north, and soon, printed cotton cloth became cheap, cheap, cheap. A yard of fabric that cost the equivalent of five dollars in 1790 was only five cents by 1840. The New England mill town of Ware, Massachusetts, turned out nearly two millions yards of cloth in one year, 1837.

From the second quarter of the nineteenth century to around 1930 or so was a good time to make quilts. Every member of the family wore shirt-weight cotton. Scraps from family sewing were cotton scraps. Yards of dress goods were yards of printed cotton, perfect for quilts. Indeed, the great flowering of American quiltmaking occurred during these years. Incredibly clever women invented (without graph paper or computers) thousands of fantastic quilt blocks, naming them marvelous names like Log Cabin, Bear Paw, Cake Stand, and Churn Dash. Just about every woman, from the time she could hold a needle, could sew. The work these gals (and a few men) turned out in the decades of the nineteenth and early twentieth centuries, whether they were stitching Album blocks in Baltimore, Feathered Stars in Kansas, or Grape Baskets in California, elevated patchwork, appliqué, and quilting itself. "The Quilt" evolved from a mere bedcover into the icon of American folk art it is today.

Hold the Nostalgia

In those days though, you had to heat your iron on a woodstove—after adding wood—visit the outhouse to powder your nose and launder your lingerie on a washboard. Your morning might start with milking a cow or assisting at childbirth. You pretty much had to date and marry a boy from the community, and family planning didn't exist. Also, from 1861 to 1865, our country was engaged in a bloody civil war. The years leading up to the War Between the States and then its aftermath were years of terrible emotional and financial hardship for almost everyone.

By the 1940s, the heyday of quilting was over. Cotton's reign was usurped by synthetic fabrics. Women were to blame, but you can't really blame them. They loved dress goods that didn't wrinkle (see ironing above) or ravel. "Homemade" quilts and other sewing seemed just so . . . homey. A blanket ordered from Sears, Roebuck, and delivered by US Parcel Post was something to show off to the neighbors. Plumbing and electricity (see outhouse above) in the home were becoming standard. Life was better, but not for the American quilt.

Cotton Went Away

The popularity of synthetics from the1930s–40s through the 1970s (think leisure suits) is why when I started making quilts, it was a really terrible time. True, the run-up to the American Bicentennial of 1976 made people nostalgic about quilts. Everybody had

two or three old ones in the closet, and some people thought the perfect thing to do to commemorate the Bicentennial was to make a quilt. The trouble was, hardly a scrap of 100% cotton could be found. Except for our blue jeans, most people hadn't a cotton garment to their name.

Despite the dearth of quilt-weight cotton, a lot of women my age—I was around 25 at the time—undaunted, used what little we could scare up to make our first quilts. But there were no books on quilting, patterns for quilts, quilting classes, quilt guilds, quilt shops, or quilting conferences. We drafted patterns (we had graph paper!), made templates from cardboard cereal boxes, cut out fabric pieces with scissors, and did much of our patchwork by hand.

The Revival Begins

Luckily, the other women in the Beginning Quilting class I requested from the ISU Home Extension Office in Winterset, Iowa—where I met Liz Porter—were not the only women in America who thought it might be fun to make a quilt. North to south, from coast to coast, interest in quiltmaking, which had actually begun in the early 1970s as part of a renewed national interest in crafts in general, was trending upward. Someone in the fabric industry noticed a surprising demand for cotton, and (hooray!) many companies began manufacturing dress-weight cottons specifically for quilts.

None of my early quilts were scrap quilts. (Scrap quilts can only be made when lots and lots and lots of fabrics are available, leftover from family garment sewing or fat quarters bought brand new.) I was lucky if I could pull together seven or eight fabrics that worked together. One stinker in those days and your quilt was not a success.

When the rotary cutter became available in the 1980s, my quilt buddies and I switched from scissors in a hot minute. With that tool in their hands, quilters every bit as clever as the pattern-inventing geniuses of a

century before came up with ways to make quilts faster and better: strip-piecing, quick-cutting, flippy corners, paper piecing. Sewing machine companies responded too, offering features to speed up the process so stitchers could devote more time to the creativity of design itself, make quilts faster, and start the next quilt sooner.

The Time Is Now

There has never, ever, been a better time to make quilts than right now. No matter what colors or styles of prints you favor, there are thousands to buy at a brick-and-mortar shop or an online one. Available to you are acrylic templates, special machine presser feet, ceramic marking tools, incredible die-cutting systems, and track lighting. You can belong to a quilt guild, actual or virtual. You can learn techniques from quilting books and magazines, from Public Television programs and online webinars, at a quilting conference, or on a quilters' cruise.

But wait, there's more! While you're quilting, you can listen to any kind of music you like, talk on your phone with anyone, anywhere, and have a pizza delivered to your door. The bathroom and the kitchen are just steps away, whether you sew in your basement, attic, or spare room. Any quilter in America who has to throw a log on the fire is probably doing so by choice.

There are plenty of good things to say about the "good old days," and I would agree, regarding quilts, "We don't make 'em like we used to." Indeed, we make them differently, and, on balance, way better. My guess is, if we could transport a quilter from any time in the American quiltmaking past to a full-service quilt shop or a national quilting event of the present, she'd be in heaven.

Marianne Fons, aside from being a legendary quilter, is also a quilt history buff and an accomplished writer. Marianne is currently working on her first novel.

6

Très Chic

MATERIALS

5 yards (4.6m) black solid for blocks, border and binding

4½ yards (4.1m) cream solid for blocks

Fons & Porter's Curved Seam Template Set or template material

4½ yards (4.1m) backing fabric

Full-size quilt batting

CUTTING

Measurements include ¼" (6mm) seam allowances. Border strips are exact length needed. You may want to cut them longer to allow for piecing variations. If not using Fons & Porter's Curved Seams Template Set, make templates from the Take-Away and Fill-In patterns at the end of this book.

From black solid, cut:

• 12 (6½" [17cm]-wide) strips. From strips, cut 72 (6½" [17cm]) A squares.

• 11 (5½" [14cm]-wide) strips. From strips, cut 72 (5½" [14cm]) B squares.

• 8 (2¼" [6cm]-wide) strips for binding.

• 8 (1¼" [3cm]-wide) strips. Piece strips to make 2 (1¼" × 74" [3cm × 188cm]) top and bottom borders and 2 (1¼" × 72½" [3cm × 184cm]) side borders.

From cream solid, cut:

• 12 (6½" [17cm]-wide) strips. From strips, cut 72 (6½" [17cm]) A squares.

• 11 (5½" [14cm]-wide) strips. From strips, cut 72 (5½" [14cm]) B squares.

Fabric Note
Moda Solids used here!

If this quilt were a person, we think she'd be living in Paris.

QUILT BY Quilty & Co.
MADE BY Nancy McNally
73½" × 73½" (187cm × 187cm)
36 (12" [30cm]) blocks
Beginner Level 3

Editor's Note: This quilt is a modern marvel—and there's nothing new about it. A classic Drunkard's Path pattern, simply rendering this quilt in black and white solid created a totally fresh look. We put Très Chic on the cover of the Mar/Apr '13 issue, and it remains one of our highest-selling issues to date. Sometimes, what's old is really, really cool again.

Block Assembly

1. Position Take-Away template on one corner of cream A square, aligning edges as shown in Cutting Diagrams A. Trace curved edge; cut on line to make 1 background piece. Make 72 cream and 72 black background pieces.

2. Position Fill-In template on 1 corner of cream B square, aligning edges as shown in Cutting Diagrams B. Trace curved edge; cut on line to make 1 quarter circle. Cut 72 cream and 72 black quarter circles using B squares.

3. Join 1 black quarter circle to 1 cream background piece to make 1 cream Block Unit (Block Unit Diagrams). Make 72 cream Block Units and 72 black Block Units.

4. Lay out 2 Cream Block Units and 2 Black Block Units as shown in Block Assembly Diagram. Join into rows; join rows to complete 1 block (Block Diagram). Make 36 blocks.

Quilt Assembly

1. Lay out blocks as shown in Quilt Top Assembly Diagram. Join your blocks into rows; join your rows to complete quilt center.

2. Add black side borders to quilt center. Then add top and bottom borders to the quilt.

Finishing

1. Divide backing into 2 (2¼ yard [2.1m]) lengths. Cut 1 piece in half lengthwise to make 2 narrow panels. Join 1 narrow panel to each side of wider panel; press seam allowances toward narrow panels.

2. Layer backing, batting, and quilt top; baste. Quilt as desired. Quilt shown was quilted with a vine design in the cream pieces and a floral design in the black pieces (Quilting Diagram).

3. Join 2¼" (6cm)-wide black strips into 1 continuous piece for straight-grain French-fold binding. Add binding to quilt. Très chic, mon chéri.

Make It Your Own

Pink and black...wow!

quilty

Designer Profile

Quilty magazine is dedicated to bringing you gorgeous quilts that you can actually make. We believe in quilts that make people smile. For more information about who we are, visit **HeyQuilty.com**.

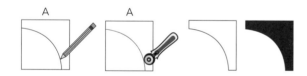

Cutting Diagrams A

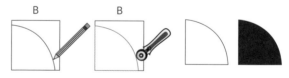

Cutting Diagrams B

Block Unit Diagrams

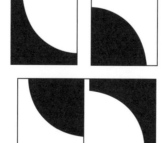

Block Assembly Diagram

Block Diagram

Learn how to sew
curved seams at
**HeyQuilty.com/
sewcurves**.

Quilting Diagram

The Quarter-Inch Seam Test

When quilters make patchwork, we sew with a ¼" (6mm) seam allowance. What does that mean? It means that the pieces of fabric that we cut have a seam allowance added on all sides. When you sew your pieces together, that ¼" (6mm) of extra fabric winds up on the back of your piecing. The result on the front is pretty patchwork that stays put. Brilliant!

It pays to be accurate with your ¼" (6mm) seam allowance. Check your work when you begin a new project and along the way in the process. Just slapping a ruler on your patchwork to check your seam allowance straight off the machine isn't really the best way to gauge accuracy, so take this seam allowance test and make sure you're flying right.

1. Cut two 2½" (6cm) squares.

2. Place squares right sides together. Sew them together with a ¼" (6mm) seam allowance. Many sewing machines can be fitted with a patchwork foot, which offers a great guide. Or use tape or a sticky note to show you how far ¼" (6mm) is from your needle (Photos A and B).

3. Open your patchwork. Press. Don't stretch out or steam and iron your fabric—just open and press to set.

4. Measure what you've got. If your seam is perfect, you should have a piece that measures 4½" (11cm) across exactly (Photo C). Why 4½" (11cm)? Well, you still have your seam allowance on either end, just waiting to be sucked up into the next piece of patchwork! When you do that on all sides, you're going to end up with 2" (5cm) finished squares.

5. If you've been sewing for awhile, help a rookie out with the ¼" (6mm) seam allowance test. Happy seams make happy quilters, who will have to be pried away from their machines. We like that.

For a great video tutorial, check this out! HeyQuilty.com/Seam

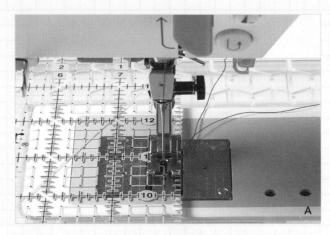

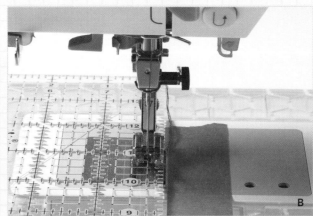

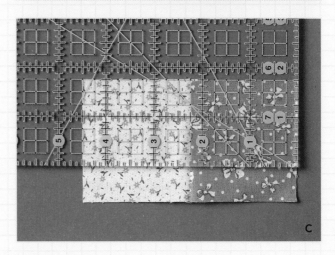

First promotional photos for *Quilty*, 2011.

The New Beginner

I grew up in rural Iowa in a town called Winterset. Not much changes in Winterset, and that can be weird, but it can also be a comfort. The town's population hovers around 5,000. The county fair each summer features the hard work of the 4-H kids. You *will* get stuck behind a tractor when driving in or out of town during harvest. There's still a big rivalry with the neighboring town's football team. There's still a Lion's Club.

You'd think that growing up in a community like that—a churchgoing, farming, small-town American community—that home economics would be a part of the high school curriculum.

Not so much.

When I was in high school in the early '90s, I had exactly one semester of home economics, and even that was broken up into two quarters separated on a rotation with Shop Class and Art. In Home Ec, we baked cookies. We learned how to write a personal check. We did sew a drawstring bag, but that was it. Why such a change from my mother's high school experience, when Home Economics was a cornerstone of every female student's high school education? Simple: Computers.

By the time I got to high school, it wasn't just computers but the Internet, too. The school board and the PTA scrambled to make sure Winterset kids learned the newfangled technology as soon as possible. Hemming pants and baking cookies gave way to learning crucial computer skills. If you didn't learn to sew at home, and you didn't learn sewing in Home Ec, where would you learn to sew? The answer: the Internet, eventually.

*   *   *

In 2010, I was attending the Spring International Quilt Market in Minneapolis, Minnesota. When I looked around at all the booths and the vendors, the quilters, the media, and, of course, the glorious quilts at the center of it all, a terrible thought occurred to me: What if no one in the next generation knows this exists? Who is teaching people coming up who have never sewn a stitch?

My cell phone was in my purse. I called my friend Sarah.

"Sarah, if you were going to make a quilt, what would you do?" I knew Sarah had never spent much time at a sewing machine.

"I'd call you or your mom," my friend said.

"Pretend you don't know me or Mom," I said. "What would you do if you wanted to make a baby quilt right now, today."

There was a brief pause. "I'd go on YouTube."

That was all I needed to hear. I pulled over into an alcove by the janitor's closet and did a YouTube search for "easy baby quilt how-to." What I found wasn't enough. There were some videos on quiltmaking instruction, but the production value was low and in the digital age, that wasn't good enough. One teacher, well-intentioned, finished her tutorial by saying, "Then just baste, quilt, and bind." I knew a beginner with no experience would have no clue what she was talking about and would never finish a quilt, much less start one.

Quilty was born that day. I pitched the idea of an online show for the true beginner. The show got the green light a few months later. That was in 2010, and well over 200 episodes have been filmed since then, which I hope is just the beginning of *Quilty*.

No matter where *Quilty* goes from here, there is a place for the new beginner.

Lolly

MATERIALS

60 (2½" [6cm]-wide) strips
assorted prints

⅝ yard (57cm) green print for
binding

5 yards (4.6m) backing fabric

Twin-size quilt batting

CUTTING

Measurements include ¼" (6mm)
seam allowances.

From green print, cut:
• 8 (2¼" [6cm]-wide) strips for
  binding.

Fabric Note
Fox Field collection
by Tula Pink for
FreeSpirit.

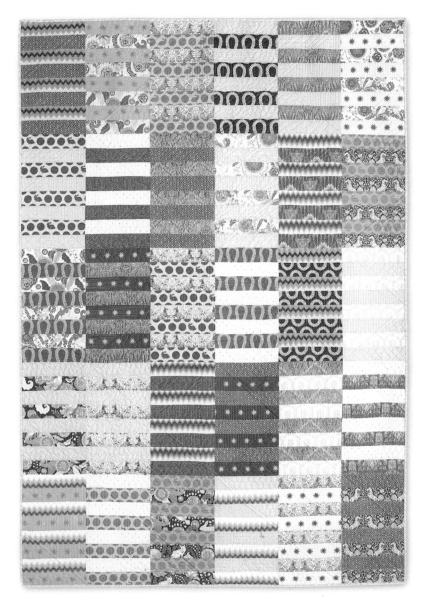

So good, you could lick it. (Don't.)

QUILT BY Tula Pink
QUILTED BY Angela Walters
57" × 80" (145cm × 203cm)
30 (9½" × 16" [24cm × 41cm]) blocks
Beginner Level 1

Editor's Note: Managing Editor Deb Finan and I saw this quilt at Fall Quilt Market and made a beeline for it; it was so perfect for *Quilty*, it was practically waving at us. Tula Pink is a phenomenal designer who uses turquoise, gold, and pink as neutrals, and in this simple strip-pieced quilt, any beginner quilter can harness the power of those gorgeous colors.

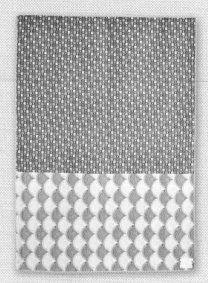

BACK STORY

When you've got fabric this luscious, use it! The backs of your quilts can be a point of interest, too.

Block Assembly

1. Referring to Strip Set Diagrams, join 2 coordinating strips length-wise. Cut strip set in half crosswise to make 2 segments.

2. Join the segments to make a 4-strip unit as shown in Block Diagrams. Cut the unit in half crosswise to make 2 segments.

3. Join the segments to make an 8-strip section. Trim sides to make a 10" × 16½" (25cm × 42cm) block. Make 30 blocks.

Quilt Assembly

1. Lay out blocks as shown in Quilt Top Assembly Diagram.

2. Join blocks into rows; join rows to complete quilt top.

Finishing

1. Divide backing into 2 (2½-yard [2.3m]) lengths. Cut 1 piece in half lengthwise to make 2 narrow panels. Join 1 narrow panel to each side of wider panel; press seam allowances toward narrow panels.

Designer Profile

Tula Pink is an illustrator, author, and fabric designer. She's most recognized for her "dark" sense of humor, a flair for hiding animals in the strangest of places (artistically, not literally!) and her unique use of color and pattern.

- -

2. Layer backing, batting, and quilt top; baste. Quilting Diagram shows suggested quilting; quilt yours as desired.

3. Join 2¼" (6cm)-wide green print strips into 1 continuous piece for straight-grain French-fold binding. Add binding to quilt.

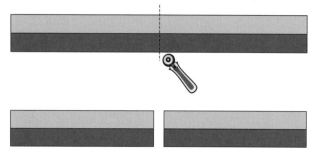

Strip Set Diagrams

Mary makes this block on *Quilty*—check it out! **HeyQuilty.com/Lolly**

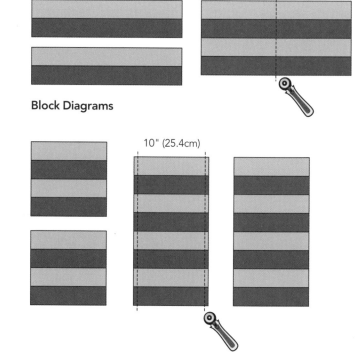

Block Diagrams

10" (25.4cm)

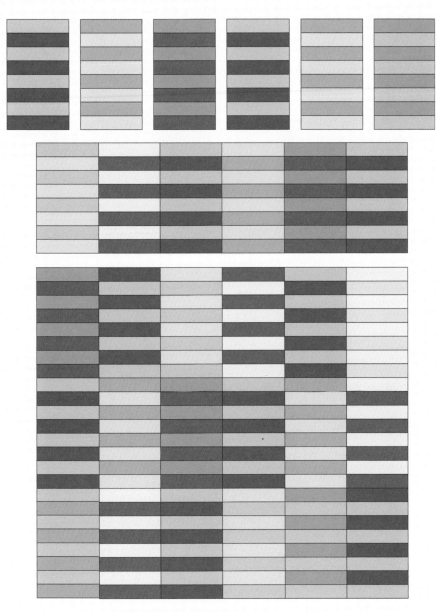

Quilt Top Assembly Diagram

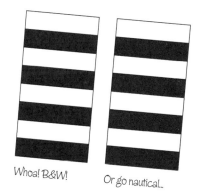

Make It Your Own

Whoa! B&W!   Or go nautical...

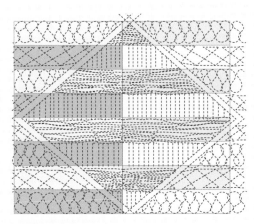

Quilting Diagram

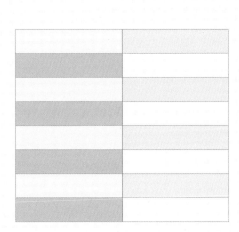

Doodle your own quilting design here.

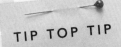
Abutting Seams

Quilty believes that striving for accuracy and quality patchwork makes for a happier sewing experience. This is an easy way to pretty up your patchwork so that you can enjoy the process even more.

Seam allowances pressed closed, to one side, are stronger than seam allowances pressed open. That's a fact. To reduce bulk, however, and achieve precision in your piecing, abut (or "lock") seams whenever possible. Check it out:

1. When possible, press your seam allowances consistently "toward the dark." That means press units with the darker seam allowance on the bottom (Photo A).

2. When you join the next unit, your seams will abut, or lock, since they are sewn facing each other. The seam allowance on the top piece goes one way, the seam allowance on the bottom goes the opposite way. This makes for a strong joint. Use a pin to hold everything together (Photo B).

3. Sew your joining seam. Set seam. Open up unit (Photo C).

4. Your patchwork is great-looking and very sturdy (Photo D).

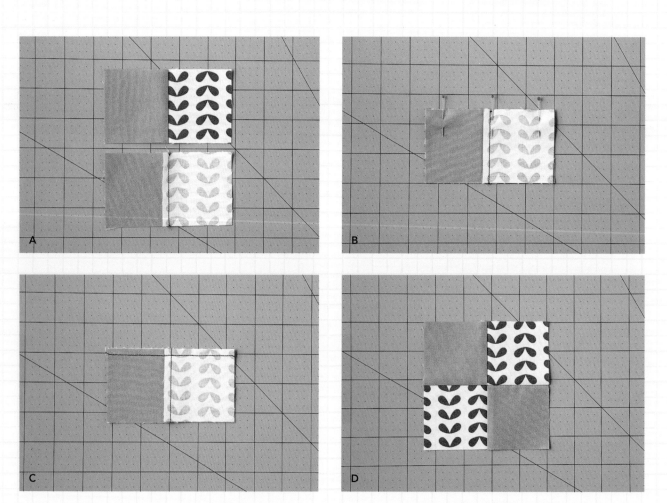

Matt Hyland

Matt Hyland, looking
pensive, hanging out
with a quilt

Matt Hyland is a sound technician
and film production professional in
Chicago.

What do you do to make _Quilty_?
I mostly focus on recording sound, but
I've also helped with designing and
setting up our sets and backgrounds.
I've worked on the show for about
three-and-a-half years, now!

**What's the hardest part of your job
as a sound technician?**
Holding the boom pole and micro-
phone steady for the duration of our
episodes, honestly. Holding your arms
above your head can be exhaust-
ing; even more so when you've got
several pounds of gear in your hands.
If my arms get tired and move, it can
diminish the sound quality, so it takes
a weird kind of concentration.

**Do you think you could make a quilt
at this point, having watched over
200 episodes?**
I honestly think I could, as long as
the blocks or patterns didn't require
advanced techniques like curved
edges or hand-appliqué. I can't prom-
ise it would be square or not fall apart,
but I could do it.

**As a non-quilter, do you "get" why
people make quilts?**
Absolutely, though I think as an
outsider the things that catch my
attention are often not what impresses
an experienced quilter. I'm more
interested in the visual of the finished
product, like interesting contrasts or
shapes or patterns that I wouldn't have
thought about. More experienced
quilters are impressed by especially
complex or difficult maneuvers, maybe
less concerned about whether the
quilt fits their "taste."

Dear Quilty:

I've always been crafty. When something sparkly catches my eye in the
store, my mind starts ticking and I ask myself, "How can I make that?"

During middle school I took a class called Life Skills (a.k.a. Home Ec)
where our class learned how to operate a sewing machine and piece a
nine-patch pillow. Feeling marvelously clever after that lesson, I dusted
off the old Universal and started to sew anything I could get my hands
on. Despite messy points, pleated backs, crooked seams, and sewing
through my right index finger, I worked tenaciously to improve my craft.
A subscription to _Love of Quilting_ magazine became my instructional and
creative ally, and when _Quilty_ came out, I rejoiced. Here it was—finally! A
celebration of modern simplicity! I'm thrilled that fresh, bold designs have
gained popularity in the past few years, and that _Quilty_ is here to help
inspire and instruct a new generation of self-taught quilters.

Sincerely,
Lauren Palmer

Hoopla

MATERIALS

½ yard (46cm) each of 15 assorted prints

2 yards (1.8m) gray solid

1 yard (.9m) teal print

5 yards (4.6m) backing fabric

Twin-size quilt batting

CUTTING

Measurements include ¼" (6mm) seam allowances.

From each print, cut:
- 2 (5¾" [14.6cm]-wide) strips. From strips, cut 10 (5¾" [14.6cm]) squares and 2 (5" [13cm]) squares. Cut 5¾" [14.6cm] squares in half diagonally in both directions to make 40 quarter-square triangles.

From gray solid, cut:
- 13 (5¾" [14.6cm]-wide) strips. From strips, cut 90 (5¾" [14.6cm]) squares. Cut squares in half diagonally in both directions to make 360 quarter-square triangles.

From teal print, cut:
- 9 (2¼" [6cm]-wide) strips for binding.

Fabric Note
Erika used the Nordika collection by Jeni Baker for Art Gallery Fabrics.

Make some noise for this gorgeous quilt.

QUILT BY Erica Jackman
67½" × 81" (171cm × 206cm)
30 (13½" [34cm]) blocks
Beginner Level 2

Editor's Note: Once you know how to make a few basic patchwork units, you can create an infinite number of quilts—how cool is that? What I loved about Hoopla—aside from its totally "now" palate—is that it's nothing but quarter-square triangles. Just good old QSTs, turned and flipped back and forth. Beginners, start hoopla-ing.

Block Assembly

1. Choose 1 set of 12 matching triangles and 1 square (Group A), 1 set of 8 matching triangles (Group B), and 12 gray solid triangles.

2. Join 2 triangles from Group A and 2 gray solid triangles as shown in Hourglass Unit Diagrams. Make 4 matching Hourglass Units.

3. In the same manner, make 2 matching Hourglass Units using 2 triangles from Group B and 2 gray solid triangles.

4. Make 2 Hourglass Units using 2 triangles from Group A and 2 triangles from Group B in each.

5. Lay out Hourglass Units and matching square as shown in Block Diagrams. Join into rows; join rows to complete 1 block. Make 30 blocks.

Quilt Assembly

1. Lay out blocks as shown in Quilt Top Assembly Diagram.

2. Join blocks into rows; join rows to complete quilt top.

Finishing

1. Divide backing into 2 (2½-yard [2.3m]) lengths. Cut 1 panel in half lengthwise to make 2 narrow panels. Join 1 narrow panel to each side of wider panel; press seam allowances toward narrow panels.

2. Layer backing, batting, and quilt top; baste. Quilting Diagram shows suggested quilting; quilt yours as desired.

3. Join 2¼" (6cm)-wide teal print strips into 1 continuous piece for straight-grain French-fold binding. Add binding to quilt.

Designer Profile

Erica Jackman of San Diego, California, is an avid quilter and blogger. You can see more of Erica's quilts at KitchenTableQuilting.com.

Watch this block being made!
HeyQuilty.com/Hoopla

 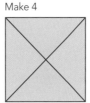 Make 4  Make 2   Make 2

Hourglass Unit Diagrams

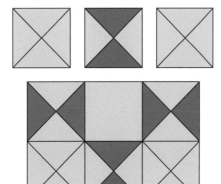

Block Assembly Diagram

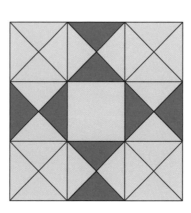

Block Diagram

Enjoy the Process
Incredible quilts are made, not born. Experiment with crazy color ideas—you might discover an extraordinary combination.

Quilt Top Assembly Design

Make It Your Own

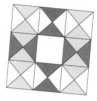

Create a different kind of "hoopla."

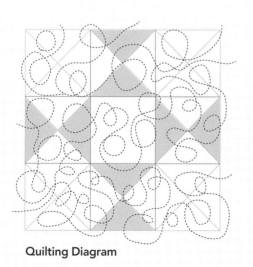

Quilting Diagram

Doodle your own quilting design here.

Getting the Hang of Quarter-Square Triangles (QSTs)

This is a quick and easy method to make Hourglass Units without cutting triangles. The Fons & Porter Quarter Inch Seam Marker helps you draw stitching lines quickly.

1. From two contrasting fabrics, cut a square 1¼" (3.1cm) larger than the desired finished size of the Hourglass Unit. For example, to make an Hourglass Unit that will finish 2" (5.1cm) our squares were cut 3¼" (8.1cm).

2. Face "pretty sides" together. Place Quarter Inch Seam Marker diagonally across the back of light square, with yellow center line positioned exactly at corners. Mark stitching guidelines along both sides of Quarter Inch Seam Marker (Photo A). Note: If you are not using the Fons & Porter Quarter Inch Seam Marker, draw a diagonal line from corner to corner across square. Then draw sewing lines on each side of the first line, ¼" (6mm) away.

3. Keeping the light square on top of your dark square, right sides facing, stitch along marked sewing lines.

4. Cut between rows of stitching to make two triangle-squares (Photo B). Press seams toward the darker fabric. If you stopped here, you'd have HSTs. But we're not done!

5. On wrong side of one triangle-square, place Quarter Inch Seam Marker diagonally, perpendicular to seam, aligning yellow center line with corners of square. Just like you

A

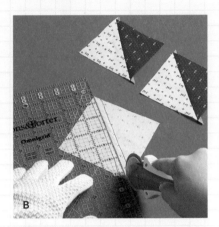

B

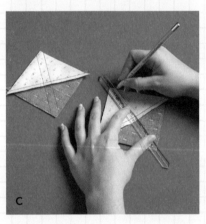

C

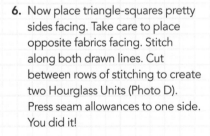

D

did before, mark stitch lines along both sides of Quarter Inch Seam Marker (Photo C). See note in step 2 if you are not using the Fons & Porter Quarter Inch Seam Marker.

6. Now place triangle-squares pretty sides facing. Take care to place opposite fabrics facing. Stitch along both drawn lines. Cut between rows of stitching to create two Hourglass Units (Photo D). Press seam allowances to one side. You did it!

Video!
For a quick video lesson, visit FonsandPorter.com/qst.

Spooly Says

"You could make quilts using just squares your whole life and enjoy it, but once you start using triangles, it's a whole new world."

Cutting QSTs

Some tools quickly become "must-haves." If you use triangles in your quilts, the Fons & Porter Half and Quarter Ruler is one of these. You'll sail through triangle cutting with this invaluable tool.

1. Place a Fons & Porter Half and Quarter Ruler on fabric strip, with line that corresponds with your strip width along bottom edge. The black tip of ruler will extend beyond top edge. Trim off end of strip along left edge of ruler.

2. Cut along right edge of ruler to make 1 quarter-square triangle (Photo A).

3. Turn ruler and align same line along top edge of strip (Photo B).

4. Repeat to cut required number of quarter-square triangles.

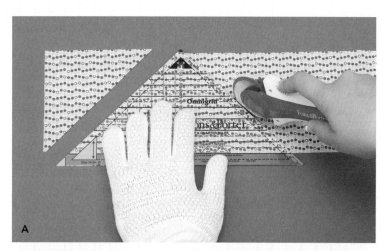

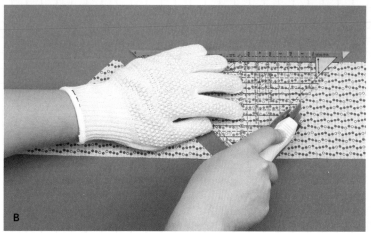

This is the Fons & Porter Half and Quarter Ruler. See one in action on *Quilty*: **HeyQuilty. com/HQRuler**.

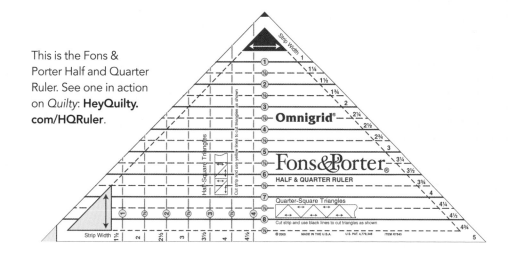

Modern Plaid

MATERIALS

4⅝ yards (4.2m) gray solid for blocks and side pieces

¾ yard (69cm) dark gray solid for binding

1⅝ yards (1.5m) aqua solid for blocks

¾ yard (69cm) light blue solid for blocks

¾ yard (69cm) medium blue solid for blocks

¼ yard (23cm) dark blue solid for blocks

7½ yards (6.9m) backing fabric

Queen-size quilt batting

CUTTING

Measurements include ¼" (6mm) seam allowances.

From gray solid, cut:
- 9 (3⅜" [9cm]-wide) strips. From strips, cut 96 (3⅜" [9cm]) squares. Cut squares in half diagonally to make 192 half-square B triangles.

- 8 (3" [8cm]-wide) strips. From strips, cut 96 (3" [8cm]) A squares.

From remainder of gray solid, cut:
- 1 (24½" [62cm]-wide) lengthwise strip. From strip, cut 1 (24½" × 100½" [62cm × 255cm]) right side piece.

- 1 (12½" [32cm]-wide) lengthwise strip. From strip, cut 1 (12½" × 100½" [32cm × 255cm]) left side piece.

From dark gray solid, cut:
- 10 (2¼" [6cm]-wide) strips for binding.

From aqua solid, cut:
- 9 (3⅜" [9cm]-wide) strips. From strips, cut 96 (3⅜" [9cm]) squares. Cut squares in half diagonally to make 192 half-square B triangles.

continued on next page

What do you get when you cross tradition with modern day? This.

QUILT BY Carl Hentsch
QUILTED BY David Hurd
73½" × 100" (187cm × 254cm)
24 (12½" [32cm]) blocks
Beginner Level 2

Editor's Note: Sometimes great quilts just fall into your lap. When Carl Hentsch pitched this quilt to us, it was one of those times. Traditional patchwork with an updated layout, an "of-the-moment" palate, and gorgeous workmanship. Team Quilty all ooh'ed and ahh'ed and Carl got a "good news!" email that day.

continued from previous page

- 8 (3" [8cm]-wide) strips. From strips, cut 96 (3" [8cm]) A squares.

From light blue solid, cut:
- 8 (3" [8cm]-wide) strips. From strips, cut 96 (3" [8cm]) A squares.

From medium blue solid, cut:
- 8 (3" [8cm]-wide) strips. From strips, cut 96 (3" [8cm]) A squares.

From dark blue solid, cut:
- 2 (3" [8cm]-wide) strips. From strips, cut 24 (3" [8cm]) A squares.

Fabric Note
Fabrics are from the Jason Yenter Modern Solids collection from In The Beginning.

Block Assembly

1. Lay out 4 light blue A squares, 4 medium blue A squares, and 1 dark blue A square as shown in Nine Patch Unit Diagrams. Join into rows; join rows to complete 1 Nine Patch Unit. Make 24 Nine Patch Units.

2. Join 1 gray B triangle and 1 aqua B triangle as shown in Triangle-Square Diagrams. Make 192 triangle-squares.

3. Join 2 triangle-squares and 1 aqua A square as shown in Side Unit Diagrams. Make 96 Side Units.

4. Lay out 4 Side Units, 1 Nine Patch Unit, and 4 gray A squares as shown in Block Diagrams. Join into rows; join rows to complete 1 block. Make 24 blocks.

Make It Your Own

Doodle your own quilting design here. We always encourage you to do your own version!

Quilt Assembly

1. Lay out blocks as shown in Quilt Top Assembly Diagram. Join blocks into vertical rows; join rows to complete center section.

2. Add left and right side pieces to center section to complete quilt top.

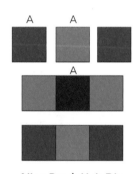

Nine Patch Unit Diagrams

Triangle-Square Diagram

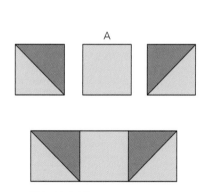

Side Unit Diagrams

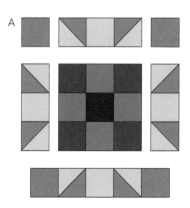

Block Diagrams

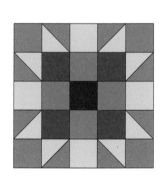

Finishing

1. Divide backing into 3 (2½-yard [2.3m]) lengths. Join panels length-wise. Seams will run horizontally.

2. Layer backing, batting, and quilt top; baste. Quilt as desired. Quilt shown was quilted with a continuous-line design in blocks and a feather design in side sections (Quilting Diagram).

3. Join 2¼" (6cm)-wide gray strips into 1 continuous piece for straight-grain French-fold binding. Add binding to quilt.

Designer Profile

Designer Carl Hentsch started quilting in the late '90s. He learned by reading and watching Fons & Porter's *Love of Quilting* on public television. He has had original designs displayed in quilt shows and traveling exhibits. Carl teaches quilting at local quilt shops, has self-published several patterns, and is the author of *Stars and Strips Forever*, published by AQS.

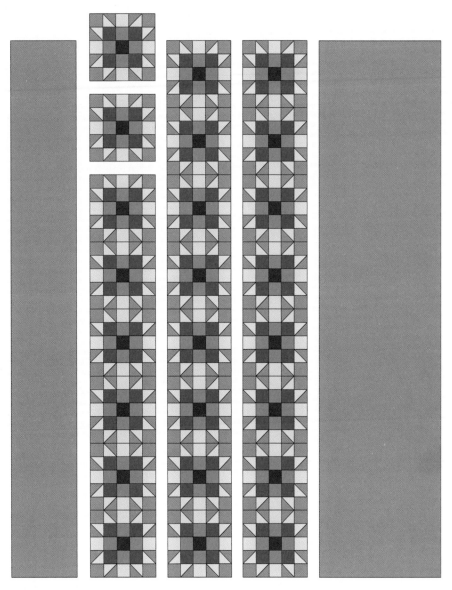

Quilt Top Assembly Diagram

Quilting Diagram

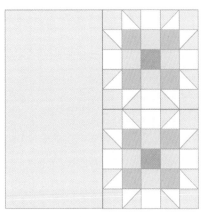

Doodle your own design here.

Cutting Straight Strips

You know how sometimes your strips have "elbows"? It happens to so many of us. Cutting straight strips is easy if you use our tried-and-true method for squaring off one end so the cut edge is at a perfect right angle to the folds.

What you need: fabric, cutting mat, cutter, and two rulers: a 6" × 12" (15cm × 30cm) and a large ruled square.

1. Fold fabric in half lengthwise, matching selvage edges. Hold fabric up, off the table, and slide the matched selvage edges in opposite directions until the fabric hangs straight, with the selvages aligned. If it hangs with a crease or buckle (Photo A), keep adjusting until it hangs smooth (Photo B).

2. Lay the folded fabric down on a cutting mat with the fold away from you and the selvages nearest you (Photo C). Fold fabric in half lengthwise, bringing selvages in alignment with the center fold (Photo D).

3. Place large ruled square on the fabric, aligning a horizontal line on the ruler with the double folded edge of the fabric nearest you, and the side of the ruler approximately ½" (13mm) from the uneven fabric end (Photo E).

4. Position the 6" × 12" (15cm × 30cm) ruler against the left edge of the square (Photo F). Now take the ruled square away but keep the 6" × 12" (15cm × 30cm) ruler in place.

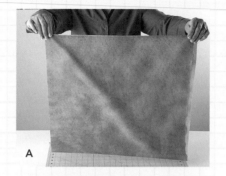

A

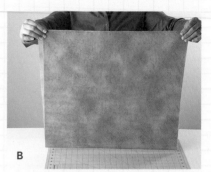

B

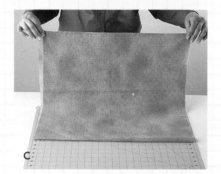

C

D

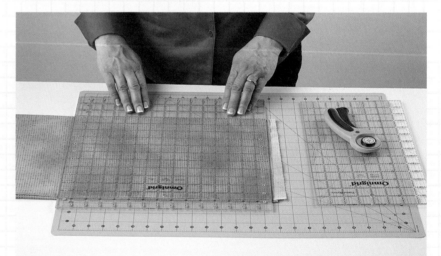

E

Enjoy the Process
Making patchwork is three things: cutting, sewing, and pressing. (Okay, four things if you count ripping.)

Video!
For all kinds of great cutting tips, techniques, and how-to's, there's no place like **QNNtv.com**.

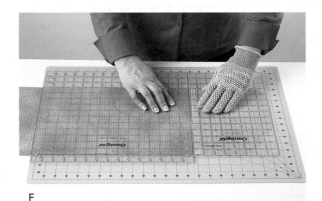

F

G

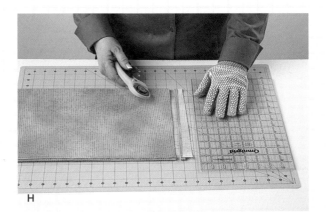

H

I

5. Cut along the edge of your ruler (Photo G), trimming away the uneven fabric edge from the end of the fabric (Photo H). You have now created a cut edge that is at a perfect 90-degree angle to the folds!

6. Reposition your ruler on the fabric so it measures the desired width (Photo I). Cut a perfectly straight strip! Continue to cut the strips needed for your project. Refold and straighten the fabric from time to time to keep your strips straight and elbow-free.

Tips

- You may need to misalign cut edges to get selvages to line up and fabric to hang straight; pressing out the center fold with your steam iron can make this easier.
- If you are right-handed, you will begin cutting strips from the left edge of the fabric. Lefty? Square off and begin from the right edge.
- As you cut strips, leave the already cut ones underneath the ruler, just moving them slightly to separate them. Leaving them on the cutting mat supports the ruler as you continue cutting.
- When cutting strips for a project, once you have your fabric positioned just right, make it a habit to cut a couple of extra strips in useful sizes, such as 2" (5cm), 2½" (6cm), and 4½" (11cm). Store these strips in plastic storage containers labeled with the strip width. Next time you want to start a new scrap quilt project, you'll have strips all ready to go!

Meet Spooly

BY MARY FONS

When you're trying something new, it's good to ask for help. But what if you don't even know the question?

At those times, the best thing that can happen is that someone—or in this case, a spool of thread—comes to the rescue. For the beginner quilter who picks up *Quilty*, there is such a hero. His name is Spooly.

When we were putting together the first issue, I thought it would be good to have some kind of narrative voice throughout the magazine to give tips and pointers as readers went along. We were forming various icons that would call attention to video links and pattern notes, but I was after something different. I wondered if a little character would be helpful. We were already planning to incorporate my doodles into the art direction of *Quilty*, so I doodled a few different ideas.

My strongest sketch was a spool of thread. There was room for a face on it (you don't really get that with a pair of scissors) and a sewing machine was way too hard to draw. I got out my colored pencils and created two complete versions of a fellow I called Spooly. I colored him blue because he's a boy (original, I know), and at the last moment, when I was filling in the black that was his open mouth, I left a little white on the bottom that gave him a tooth. I thought he looked pretty cute.

The whole time I was drawing this cartoon, however, I believed he was a prototype. I figured he would be ren-dered again by a real illustrator on a fancy computer and my sketch would simply be something from which to work. As it turns out, there was zero budget for illustrations. Anything I drew for the magazine was going to be the drawing used in the magazine, so ready or not, Spooly was going into *Quilty* as drawn.

People loved Spooly from the start. We get reader email about this or that and frequently a "p.s., I love Spooly!!!" comes below the signature. When Spooly started appearing on the cover and getting actual fan mail addressed to him, I realized a star had been born.

The truth is, a cartoon character is a tricky thing. You don't want to seem patronizing—*Quilty* is a magazine for adults, after all. And without a real reason to be there, Spooly would be frivolous, even ridiculous. But the truth is, the little guy really does help you make quilts. The "Spooly Says" tips are solid and deliver information in a useful, bite-sized way that would be hard to include otherwise. No one wants a big block of copy invading their pattern pages. Spooly rolls in, does his thing, and then rolls right out.

Who knows what the future holds for Spooly? A record deal? Scorcese picture? Perhaps a line of pincushions is the best place to start. Whatever happens, readers can trust the one-toothed wonder will be hanging out in *Quilty* as long as *Quilty* is around: he knows a good gig when he sees it.

Spooly, Our Star

Courtney Kraig

What does an art director do?
I consider myself a visual problem-solver, and I like to push the quilt envelope by creating fun, clean, modern design layouts for *Quilty* magazine. I take what the brilliant and talented editors dream up and translate it into what you see on the page. I also drink a lot of coffee.

What's different about *Quilty* compared to other quilting and craft magazines you've worked on?
I think *Quilty* appeals to the "new-to-quilting" quilter because it's quirky and fun but at the same time maintains simple, informative instructions and tips that a beginner can relate to and easily learn from.

How would you describe the overall tone of *Quilty*, art-wise or feeling-wise?
Quilty is like your bestie: fun and always there to help you out. It's cutting-edge and on trend, too. You just can't help wanting to be around this magazine!

You made the magazine team adorable Spooly pincushions for Christmas one year. Do you have any idea what that did to his ego?? He thinks he should be on billboards now!! What were you thinking??
I love to make crazy gifts for people especially around the holidays and one day he just popped into my head. I had this rather large box full of scrap felt (don't ask) so I did what anyone would have done in this situation: I created little Spooly dude!

You're in Colorado. Deb's in Pennsylvania. There's the Iowa branch. Mary is who-knows-where at any given time. Do you ever just wish you could all be in the same spot to make the magazine?
It would be fabulous to work in the same location with Team Quilty! On the other hand, I think we would miss out on all that everyone brings to the table from these different locations. We're lucky to have such a broad perspective with all the traveling and visits to much of the quilting community throughout the country. It helps *Quilty* offer so much more and keeps it fresh and energized. So I'll stay put for now!

Sleepy Baby

MATERIALS

½ yard (46cm) each of white, navy, and blue prints

⅜ yard (34cm) of brown print

3⅛ yards (3.1m) of green print

2¾ yards (2.5m) of backing fabric

Crib-size quilt batting

CUTTING

Measurements include ¼" (6mm) seam allowances. Pattern for diamonds (Sleepy Baby Template) is at the end of this book.

From each of white, navy, and blue prints, cut:
• 18 diamonds.

From brown print, cut:
• 9 diamonds.

From green print, cut:
• 80 diamonds.

• 6 (2¼" [6cm]-wide) strips for binding.

Fabric Note
E-I-E-I-O by Dear Stella.

The sheep are jumpin'...

QUILT BY Quilty and Co.
40½" × 54¼" (103cm × 138cm)
Beginner Level 3

Editor's Note: There's a joke in the quilt world that the baby quilt is "the gateway drug," meaning that many of us get a taste of quiltmaking with a small baby quilt and then need more...more! We run a great baby quilt in each issue of *Quilty* because a) we know people want them and b) we love babies. We loved the fabric in this quilt—those little sheep!—and that it was non-gender specific. To fall in love with this one, any sleepy baby will do.

Quilt Assembly

1. Lay out diamonds as shown in Quilt Top Assembly Diagram.

2. Join diamonds into diagonal rows; join rows to complete quilt top.

3. Trim sides, top, and bottom as shown.

Finishing

1. Divide backing into 2 (1⅜-yard [1.3m]) lengths. Join panels lengthwise. Seam will run horizontally.

2. Layer backing, batting, and quilt top; baste. Quilt as desired. Quilt shown was quilted with allover meandering design of loops and animals (Quilting Diagram).

3. Join green 2¼" (6cm)-wide strips into 1 continuous piece for straight-grain French-fold binding. Add binding to quilt.

Make It Your Own

"Tutti Frutti"

Quilt Top Assembly Diagram

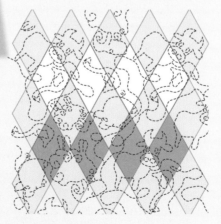

Quilting Diagram

Doodle your own quilting design here.

34

Fussy Cutting

Spooly Says
"Your fabric will look like Swiss cheese. Brace yourself."

If you've ever cut out a single flower from a larger print, you've done what's called "fussy cutting." Here is a way to get lots of specific pieces more quickly.

1. Make a plastic template that gives you at least a ¼" (6mm) on all sides of your desired cut-out portion.

2. Position template on your desired fabric motif (Photo A). Draw around template and cut on line or cut around template with rotary cutter.

3. Check your work. Place cut-out motif on top of the fabric, right sides up, aligning your cut-out with the print. If properly aligned, you will barely be able to see the cut piece (Photo B).

4. Cut around your cut-out with scissors to make an identical piece (Photo C). Be careful not to cut your pattern piece.

5. Repeat as many times as you need to so you can get that bird! (Or whatever shape you're after.)

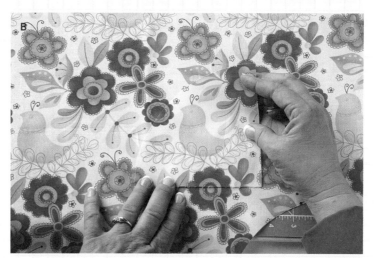

Video!
Check out a cute watermelon table runner that uses fussy cutting. Sandy Gervais will show you how on "Quilt With the Stars!" **QNNtv.com/SandyG**

On "Inspiration"

BY MARY FONS

When I was in junior and senior high school, I spent a lot of time reading fashion magazines. Though my adolescent self-image probably suffered a little, my imagination benefitted—and that meant my love of magazines was forever cemented. I loved the photo shoot locations, the colors of the clothes, the exuberance behind everything. I loved the art direction, the styling, the layouts, and the fonts, though I didn't know any of those terms back then.

I noticed that the last page of a magazine (fashion and otherwise), right before the back cover stock, was special real estate. This single page would usually offer a recurring feature that felt like a bonus, or a post-script. It could be a brief celebrity profile, a "last look" at the "it" bag that season, a trend to look out for, or a flashback to a vintage issue.

When the dream job of editing a magazine became a reality, I knew I wanted to do a "last look" page. What would be Quilty's wave goodbye each issue? What would be the "until we meet again" sentiment on that penultimate page?

As a quilter, I look for inspiration everywhere—not just in quilts. I see quilting motifs in henna tattoos, patchwork patterns in cornfields, and frequently wish some cool wallpaper would have a cotton fabric version.

That was it!

The final page of Quilty magazine could offer a kind of "Until we meet again, here's something to think about" page with a round-up of sorts of (typically) non-quilt inspiration for our quilts. Indeed, henna tattoos, cornfields, and wallpaper have all been featured on the "Inspiration" back page of Quilty, in addition to postage stamps, floor tile, butterflies, and much more.

Do people take the Inspiration page literally and go find floor tiles to copy and translate into quilts? Maybe—and that would be great! I think it's much more likely that the back page offers a way to look at the art we make in a broader way and encourages quilters to put the world around them into their quilts.

Put another way: If seeing a picture of a tulip field in Denmark reminds you that you love red and yellow and the next time you're ready for a new project you make a beeline for your red and yellow scraps, well, the Inspiration page is doing exactly what it was meant to do.

Mary and Rebecca between episodes, Chicago, 2014.

Deb Finan, who was probably solving nine problems in her head when this picture was taken.

Deb Finan

Expert quilter and accomplished editor Deb Finan serves as Managing Editor of *Quilty* magazine.

What makes *Quilty* different from other quilting magazines?
Quilty takes a "free to be me" approach to quilting, encouraging quilters to experiment with color and design, while still learning sound quilting skills.

You do so many jobs on a lot of different titles at Fons & Porter. What's your favorite part of what you do?
It would be hard to narrow that down to one thing. I have loved quilts and fabric since I was a small child, so working with quilts everyday is a dream job. I also enjoy writing instructions, seeing new fabric collections, going to Market, watching the industry grow… It's all exciting!

If anyone knows, it's you: What makes a great quilt?
A great quilt is one the speaks to you. It might not be pretty to someone else or made well according to the quilt police, but if you love it, it's a great quilt.

A Quick Quilter's Glossary: 10 Words You Should Know

Knowing what someone means when they say "selvage" or "bias" is important because the more you know, the better your quilts get.

Appliqué: Ornamental needlework in which pieces of fabric are sewn or fused onto a larger piece of fabric. Done by hand, by machine, or with fusible materials, appliqué is often combined with pieced blocks in quiltmaking.

Batting: The middle layer of the quilt sandwich that gives a quilt its relative thickness. Batting can be cotton, polyester, silk, wool, or a blend.

Bias: See Grain.

Feed Dogs: The mechanism in a sewing machine that feeds fabric under the needle.

Grain: Direction of threads in a piece of fabric. There are three directions possible. Lengthwise grain runs the length of the fabric as it comes off the bolt. Considered straight-grain, with no give or stretch. The crosswise grain, also straight, runs from selvage to selvage; offers some give. Bias grain runs diagonally across the lengthwise and crosswise grain; offers maximum stretch and give. Try pulling a piece of fabric from the two diagonally opposite corners. Notice the stretch. That's bias.

Loft: The puffiness or thickness of your batting. Higher loft = puffier, thicker. Tip: Polyester typically has a higher loft than cotton.

Rotary Cutter: A patchworker's handheld tool used to cut fabric; similar in appearance to a pizza cutter, with a round blade rotating on an axle. Rotary cutters must be used in conjunction with a rotary cutting mat and Plexiglas ruler.

Sashing: Fabric separating blocks in a quilt top.

Selvage: An edge produced on woven fabric during manufacture that prevents it from unraveling. Typically ½ to ⅓ of an inch (13mm –13mm); usually trimmed and not sewn into a quilt. May be spelled "Selvedge."

Templates: A shaped piece of plastic in quiltmaking used as a pattern for cutting out shapes or for transferring quilting lines to a quilt top.

Irish Chain

MATERIALS

3 yards (2.7m) red solid for blocks and binding

5 yards (4.6m) white solid for blocks and border

5¼ yards (4.8m) backing fabric

Twin-size quilt batting

CUTTING

Measurements include ¼" (6mm) seam allowances. Border strips are exact length needed. You may want to cut them longer to allow for piecing variations.

From red solid, cut:

• 30 (2½" [6cm]-wide) strips. Piece 7 strips to make 2 (2½" × 74½" [6cm × 189cm]) side middle borders and 2 (2½" × 58½" [6cm × 149cm]) top and bottom middle borders. Remaining strips are for strip sets.

• 9 (2¼" [6cm]-wide) strips for binding.

From white solid, cut:

• 6 (6½" [17cm]-wide) strips for strip sets.

• 8 (5½" [14cm]-wide) strips. Piece strips to make 2 (5½" × 78½" [14cm × 199cm]) side outer borders and 2 (5½" × 68½" [14cm × 174cm]) top and bottom outer borders.

• 31 (2½" [6cm]-wide) strips. Piece 7 strips to make 2 (2½" × 70½" [6cm × 179cm]) side inner borders and 2 (2½" × 54½" [6cm × 138cm]) top and bottom inner borders. Remaining strips are for strip sets.

Fabric Note

Fabrics in the quilt shown are brought to you by Christa's fabric stash!

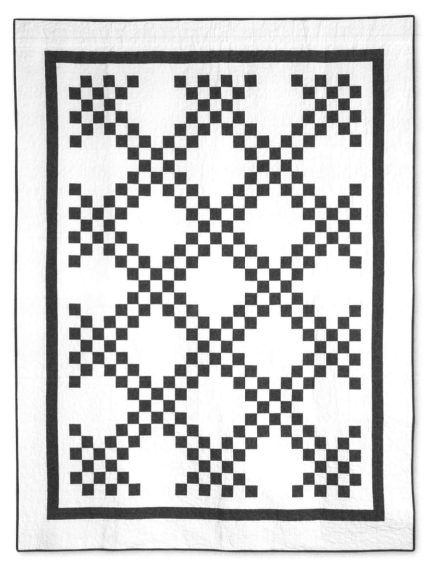

Red and white quilts are classic Americana. In this brilliant but simple design, the luck of the Irish Chain is perfected for the 21st century quilter. Modern, traditional…or both?

QUILT BY Christa Smith
68" × 88" (173cm × 224cm)
35 (10" [25cm]) blocks
Beginner Level 2

Editor's Note: In the mid-1800s, the red and white quilt came into fashion, big time. Patchwork in America was enjoying tremendous popularity already, but then came access to colorfast red fabric. Hallelujah! The quilters in those days knew beauty when they saw it: almost 200 years later, the red and white quilt is as gorgeous and elegant as it's ever been, perfect in any home.

Block Assembly

1. Join 3 white (2½" [6cm] wide) strips and 2 red strips as shown in Strip Set #1 Diagram. Make 4 Strip Set #1. From strip sets, cut 54 (2½" [6cm]-wide) #1 segments. We hope you like squares: there are many to cut for this quilt!

2. Join 3 red strips and 2 white (2½" [6cm]-wide) strips as shown in Strip Set #2 Diagram. Make 3 Strip Set #2. From strip sets, cut 36 (2½" [6cm]-wide) #2 segments.

3. Join 2 red strips and 1 white (6½" [17cm]-wide) strip as shown in Strip Set #3 Diagram. Make 3 Strip Set #3. From strip sets, cut 34 (2½" [6cm]-wide) #3 segments.

4. Join 2 white (2½" [6cm]-wide) strips and 1 white (6½" [17cm]-wide) strip as shown in Strip Set #4 Diagram. Make 3 Strip Set #4. From strip sets, cut 17 (6½" [17cm]-wide) #4 segments.

5. Lay out 3 #1 segments and 2 #2 segments as shown in Block 1 Assembly Diagrams. Join segments to complete 1 Block 1 (Block 1 Diagram). Make 18 Block 1.

6. Lay out 2 #3 segments and 1 #4 segment as shown in Block 2 Assembly Diagram. Join segments to complete 1 Block 2 (Block 2 Diagram). Make 17 Block 2.

Go team!

Go-Go

Make It Your Own

2½" (6cm)

Strip Set #1 Diagram

2½" (6cm)

Strip Set #2 Diagram

2½" (6cm)

Strip Set #3 Diagram

6½" (17cm)

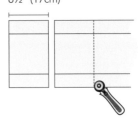

Strip Set #4 Diagram

Block 1 Assembly Diagrams

Block 1 Diagram

Block 2 Assembly Diagram

Block 2 Diagram

Tip Top Tip

When joining strips for strip sets, alternate sewing direction from strip to strip. This keeps strip sets straight.

Quilt Assembly

1. Lay out blocks as shown in Quilt Top Assembly Diagram. Join into rows; join rows to complete quilt center.

2. Add white side inner borders to quilt center.

3. Add top and bottom inner borders to quilt.

4. Repeat for red middle borders and white outer borders.

Finishing

1. Divide backing into 2 (2⅝-yard [2.4m]) lengths. Cut 1 piece in half lengthwise to make 2 narrow panels. Join 1 narrow panel to each side of wider panel; press seam allowances toward narrow panels.

2. Layer backing, batting, and quilt top; baste.

3. Quilt as desired. Quilt shown was quilted with allover meandering (Quilting Diagram).

4. Join 2¼" (6cm)-wide red strips into 1 continuous piece for straight-grain French-fold binding. Add binding to quilt.

Designer Profile

Christa Smith's appreciation for everything vintage, traditional, and homemade made it natural for her to learn the art of quilting. Over the 13 years she's been quilting, Smith has become a teacher to many; when her family was suddenly transplanted from California to Tennessee, economics drove the creation of a quilt-related family business. Now the Smith family owns and operates Cotton Berry Quilts where they sell homemade custom quilts and offer longarm quilting services.

For more information about Christa, visit CottonBerryQuilts.com.

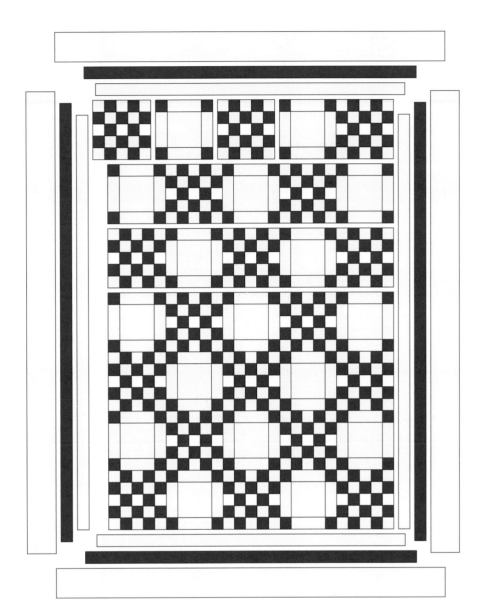

Quilt Top Assembly Diagram

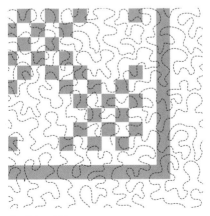

Quilting Diagram

Enjoy the Process
If you choose to turn your quilt's binding by hand (the preferred *Quilty* way) you'll need a thimble. Try out different sizes and styles before you buy: a too-tight thimble is like a too-tight shoe. Boo.

Strip Sets

If you need lots of "twosies" or "three-sies," a strip set is a real pal. Here are tips for making them work for you.

1. Join two strips together sewing your very best quarter-inch (6mm) seam. Set your seam (Photo A).

2. Press open and then join your third strip to the opposite side (Photo B).

3. Using your rotary cutter, mat, and ruler, cut your strip set into the units you need (Photo C).

Tips

- You may be tempted to cut stacks of strip sets, but beware: the seams make it hard to cut multiples accurately.
- When pressing open your long seam, use a light touch. Long strips can get bent out of shape easily.

BEE HAPPY

We show you how in this video!
HeyQuilty.com/Seams

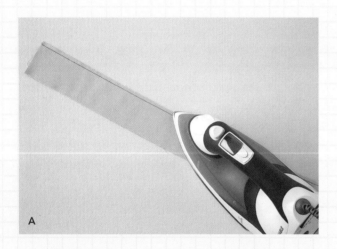

A

B

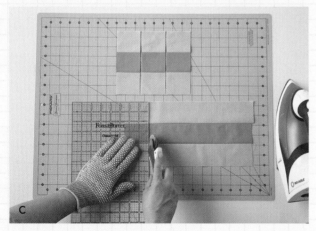

C

© 2012 M.K.F.

Marianne Fons, legendary quilter, aspiring novelist, mother, and all-around incredible human.

Marianne Fons

What do you do to make *Quilty* happen?

Luckily, all I have to do (mostly) is show up in Chicago on the day my episodes are scheduled for taping. Sometimes, I do some of the prep work for the episode content. Also, I sometimes look through my "archives" at home, and bring something neat along, like a photo of Mary when she was a kid, or some quilts from my stash.

Love of Quilting and *Quilty* are different things, conceptually, even though both brands are trying to help people make quilts.

What's different about working on *Quilty*, as compared to, say, doing stuff like TV for *LoQ*?

Well, of course I am a huge fan of public television, and I know people everywhere have learned a ton of great techniques from me and the others who host and guest on *Love of Quilting* episodes. *Quilty* also offers fabulous information about quilts and quilting techniques, but the pieces of content are shorter, more like a yummy piece of chocolate than a three-layer cake, to use a dessert metaphor. What I love best about *Quilty* is that because it's not public television, Mary and I can cut up more, which we do.

One thing I feel really proud about is that you always say how much fun you have on the *Quilty* set. Tell me, what's so fun about *Quilty*?

See my answer to the above question. To elaborate, everything at *Quilty* is, er, casual. There are great opportunities for cracking the crew up at *Quilty*.

What advice do you have for beginner quilters?

Make the quilts you want to make, not the quilts you or someone else thinks you should make. Bear in mind that once you can handle the basic skills, you will never, ever be bored for the rest of your life!

Hitchens

MATERIALS

2¼ yards (2.1m) burgundy solid for blocks and binding

1⅞ yards (1.7m) indigo-and-white print

⅜ yard (34cm) each of 9 assorted red prints

7½ yards (6.9m) backing fabric (if fabric is 44" (112cm) wide, you'll need only 5 yards [4.6m])

Queen-size quilt batting

CUTTING

Measurements include ¼" (6mm) seam allowances.

From burgundy solid, cut:
- 4 (12½" [32cm]-wide) strips. From strips, cut 12 (12½" [32cm]) squares. Cut squares in half diagonally to make 24 half-square triangles.

- 9 (2¼" [6cm]-wide) strips for binding.

From indigo-and-white print, cut:
- 5 (12½" [32cm]-wide) strips. From strips, cut 13 (12½" [32cm]) squares. Cut squares in half diagonally to make 26 half-square triangles (1 is extra).

From assorted red prints, cut a total of:
- 25 (12½" [32cm]) squares. Cut squares in half diagonally to make 50 half-square triangles (1 is extra).

Fabric Note
Mary used red fabric by Rowan, Westminster, and others. Burgundy by Moda, indigo-and-white print by In The Beginning.

Made with love for a friend.

QUILT BY Mary Fons
QUILTED BY LuAnn Downs
80½" (204cm) square
Beginner Level 1

Editor's Note: This quilt was made in homage to someone who passed away. When I saw what the stylists and the photographer had done with the shot, I probably made a noise that sounded like the honk of a goose. That dog! So gorgeous, so perfect—and sad. This shot is a testament to the talent of the people who make magazines at Fons & Porter.

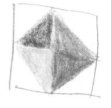

Make your QSTs say "ME!"

Block Assembly

1. Join 1 burgundy solid triangle and 1 red print triangle as shown in Triangle-Square Diagrams. Make 24 burgundy/red triangle-squares.

2. In the same manner, make 25 triangle-squares using 1 indigo-and-white triangle and 1 red print triangle in each.

3. Trim each triangle-square to 12" (30cm).

Quilt Assembly

1. Lay out triangle-squares as shown in Quilt Top Assembly Diagram.

2. Join into rows; join rows to complete quilt top.

Finishing

1. Divide backing into 3 (2½-yard [2.3m]) lengths. Cut 1 piece in half lengthwise to make 2 narrow panels. Join wider panels to sides of 1 narrow panel; press seam allowances toward wider panels. Remaining narrow panel is extra.

2. Layer backing, batting, and quilt top; baste. Quilt as desired. Quilt shown was quilted with a diagonal grid (Quilting Diagram).

3. Join 2¼" (6cm)-wide black strips into 1 continuous piece for straight-grain French-fold binding. Add binding to quilt.

Make 24

Make 25

Triangle-Square Diagrams

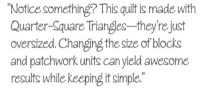

Spooly Says

"Notice something? This quilt is made with Quarter-Square Triangles—they're just oversized. Changing the size of blocks and patchwork units can yield awesome results while keeping it simple."

Designer Profile

Mary Fons is the editor of *Quilty* magazine in addition to hosting the weekly show on QNNtv.com. She is co-host of *Love of Quilting* on PBS with her mom, Marianne Fons, and has the pleasure of interviewing quilt industry leaders on "Quilt With the Stars." Mary enjoys traveling, shopping, eating, and dancing. She lives in downtown Chicago. For more information about Mary, visit MaryFons.com.

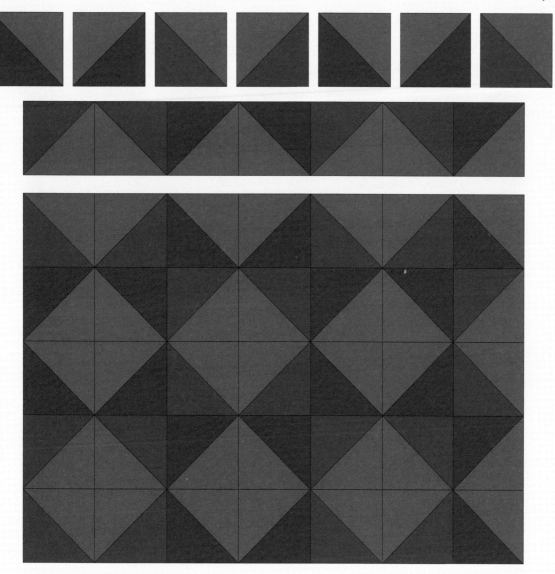

Quilt Top Assembly Diagram

Quilting Diagram

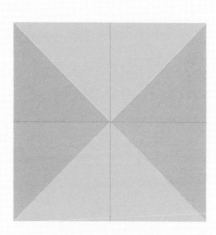

Doodle your own quilting design here.

Watch QSTs in action!
HeyQuilty.com/QSTs

Making a Design Wall

Felt!

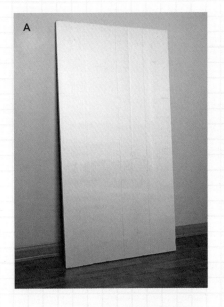

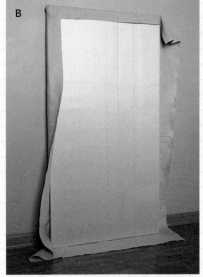

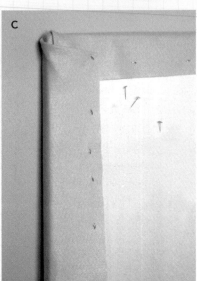

At *Quilty*, we believe a design wall is as essential to the quiltmaking process as fabric. To really "see" what you're doing and track your progress, a design wall is an invaluable tool that allows you to tack up blocks and pieces as you go. Your quilts will never be the same—they'll be better.

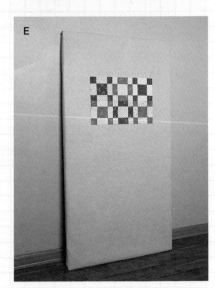

1. Make friends with someone who owns a truck.

2. Get a piece of foam insulation board from the hardware store. Get it home in your friend's truck. Most insulation boards come in 4' × 8' (122cm × 244cm) sheets. Cut to size as needed with a craft knife or box cutter (Photo A).

3. Cover with a neutral colored felt; secure with T-pins. You'd think staples would work, but they don't. Trust us (Photos B and C).

4. Prop against wall or secure onto wall however you see fit. Throw those blocks and pieces up there and go, baby, go! (Photos D and E).

Heather Kinion

Heather Kinion, a force of *Quilty* nature

Heather Kinion is a quilter and professional sewist living in Chicago.

What do you to do make *Quilty*?
I do lots of things for the show and the magazine: sewing, production work, and I've been a guest several times. Several of my quilts have been featured in the magazine, as well.

How long have you been making quilts?
I've been quilting since 2009, but learned to sew when I was in first or second grade.

How has working on the show impacted your own quiltmaking?
I've definitely test-driven a bunch of "new to me" techniques, including paper-piecing, which was an episode I was going to tape with you, Mary! I'm not sure I would've gotten around to trying on my own and that has definitely inspired and shaped the way I choose to put my quilts together. I tend to be drawn to simpler blocks in my own quilts, those that let colors of fabrics shine on their own. But many of the Blocks-a-Go-Go shows use much more complicated blocks and I've

noticed them creeping into my own work. And starch. I use starch now. Sometimes.

What does *Quilty* do well?
The series is great at being a reliable source for tutorials on techniques or blocks. Mary is always really careful to give and use best practices, and she's always asking me to think through/look out for pitfalls for newbie quilters and sewists when I'm working on stepouts. I've watched some other online tutorials where I think, "Yeah, that method gets you to your end result faster, but those blocks are going to be stretchy bias messes if you don't know what you're doing." Plus, the magazine and the show showcase modern fabrics and modern quilts, which is great.

Your family flipped when you were first published in *Quilty*. Tell me what that was like.
I'm fairly certain some of my family members now think I'm famous, which is hilarious, and a lot of non-quilters who are related to me own that issue. It's very sweet of them. My mom even found the magazine at her grocery store and like, dragged it around from checker to checker—and the pharmacist and the latte lady—to show them my quilt. So now the grocery store people congratulate me when I'm in the store with her.

Dear *Quilty*:

As a teacher, author and fabric designer since 1975, I've seen many quilt styles, fabric trends and traditional dissemination of quilt related information (hard copy magazines and TV shows) embraced by quilt makers and sewists undergo many changes with the advent of personal video and computer technologies.

Quilty speaks to the new generation of computer savvy quilt makers and those of us who value the benefits of online learning and teaching alike. Online learning is convenient for the student's schedule while the teacher is able to reach an unlimited number of students at any time of the day. *Quilty* is a win/win enterprise!

I am a *Quilty* follower because I want my classes, projects and fabrics to appeal to quilt makers and sewists of all ages and disciplines. A teacher needs to stay fresh with current trends and techniques. *Quilty* provides that for me.

Sincerely,
Linda Carlson

Geese Migration

MATERIALS

1¾ yards (1.6m) beige solid

1 fat eighth* each of 25 assorted solids or 25 (10" [25cm]) squares in gray, green, teal, navy, tan, blue, purple, lavender, red, orange, tan, and taupe

Assorted print scraps to coordinate with solids, total 375 (2½" [6cm]) squares and 125 (2½" × 4½" [6cm × 11cm]) rectangles

⅝ yard [57cm] olive print for binding

4 yards (3.7m) backing fabric

Twin-size quilt batting

*Fat eighth = 9" × 20" (23cm × 51cm)

CUTTING

Measurements include ¼" (6mm) seam allowances.

From beige solid, cut:
- 2 (18¼" [46cm]-wide) strips. From strips, cut 3 (18¼" [46cm]) squares and 2 (9½" [24cm]) squares. Cut 18¼" (46cm) squares in half diagonally in both directions to make 12 side setting triangles. Cut 9⅜" (24cm) squares in half diagonally to make 4 corner setting triangles.

- 12 (1½" [4cm]-wide) strips. From 9 strips, cut 2 (1½" × 32½" [4cm × 83cm]) sashing strips and 20 (1½" × 10½" [4cm × 27cm]) sashing strips. Piece remaining strips to make 2 (1½" × 54½" [4cm × 138cm]) sashing strips.

From each of 25 solids, cut:
- 10 (2½" [6cm]) squares.

From assorted prints, cut a total of:
- 25 sets of 15 (2½" [6cm]) squares to coordinate with each solid.

continued on next page

Fly right.

QUILT BY Cynthia Brunz
62" × 62" (157cm × 157cm)
25 (10" [25cm]) blocks
Beginner Level 3

Editor's Note: Sometimes, you know you've got a cover girl on your hands. With Geese Migration, Cynthia made the perfect "*Quilty* quilt." It's simple—just flying geese and patches—it's scrappy, and it makes quilters everywhere, beginner or not, look like the coolest people on the planet. This is what quilts look like in the 21st century? Sign me up.

continued from previous page

- 25 sets of 5 (2½" × 4½" [6cm × 11cm]) rectangles to coordinate with each solid.

From olive print, cut:
- 7 (2¼" [6cm]-wide) strips for binding.

Fabric Note
Moda Solids used here!

Make It Your Own

For your cabin.

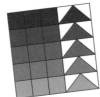

For your clubhouse.

Block Assembly

1. Place 1 solid square atop 1 print rectangle, right sides facing. Stitch from corner to corner as shown in Flying Geese Unit Diagrams. Trim ¼" (6mm) beyond stitching. Press open to reveal triangle. Repeat with matching square on opposite end of rectangle to complete 1 Flying Geese Unit. Make 5 Flying Geese Units using same solid for squares and assorted prints for rectangles.

2. Referring to Block Assembly Diagrams, lay out Flying Geese Units and 15 assorted print squares. Arrange Flying Geese Units and squares to achieve a pleasing color balance.

3. Join Flying Geese Units to make a row. Join squares into rows.

4. Join rows to complete 1 block (Block Diagram).

5. In the same manner, working on 1 block at a time, make 24 more blocks.

Quilt Assembly

1. Lay out blocks, sashing strips, and setting triangles as shown in Quilt Top Assembly Diagram.

2. Join into rows; join rows to complete quilt top.

Designer Profile

Cynthia Brunz loves color and fabric. She favors making scrappy quilts and writes about quilting with scraps on her blog QuiltingIsMoreFunThan-Housework.blogspot.com.

Finishing

1. Divide backing into 2 (2-yard [1.8m]) lengths. Join panels lengthwise.

2. Layer backing, batting, and quilt top; baste. Quilting Diagram shows suggested quilting; quilt yours as desired.

3. Join 2¼" (6cm)-wide olive print strips into 1 continuous piece for straight-grain French-fold binding. Add binding to quilt.

Flying Geese Unit Diagrams

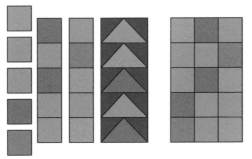

Block Assembly Diagrams

Block Diagram

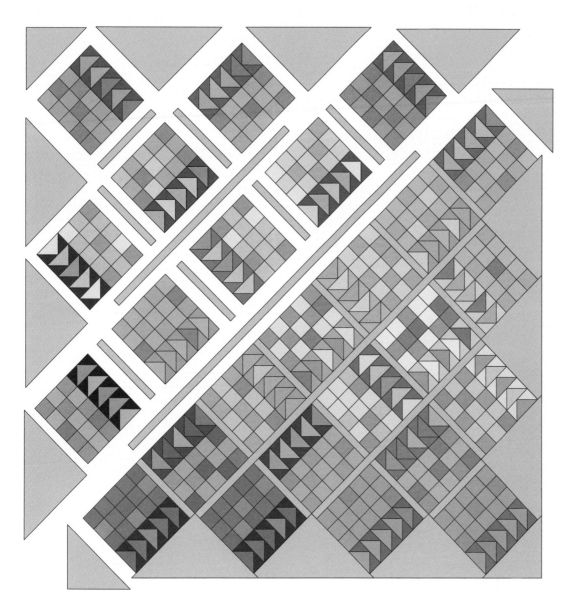

Quilt Top Assembly Diagram

Note
Refer to quilt photo for fabric placement guidance.

Quilting Diagram

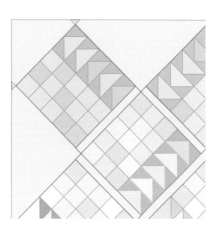

Doodle your own quilting design here.

This quilt uses lots of colors, no? Get tips on building your personal stash in this must-see episode: **HeyQuilty.com/StashTips.**

Flying Geese

The Fons & Porter Flying Geese Ruler is super handy for cutting triangles for Flying Geese units. Both the large quarter-square triangles and the smaller half-square triangles can be cut from the same width strips.

1. To cut the large quarter-square tri-angle, select black line on ruler that corresponds to the desired finished size of your Flying Geese Unit.

2. Follow across black line to right edge of ruler. Cut a fabric strip the width indicated. For example, to cut the large triangle for a 3" × 6" (8cm × 15cm) finished size Flying Geese Unit, cut a 3½" (9cm)-wide strip.

3. Cut quarter-square triangles as shown in Photo A, alternately placing the black cutting guideline along bottom edge of strip and then along top edge of the strip (Photo A).

4. To cut the corresponding smaller half-square triangles, select the yellow line that corresponds to the desired finished size Fly-ing Geese Unit.

5. Follow across that yellow line to left edge of ruler and cut a fabric strip the width indicated. For exam-ple, to cut the small triangles for a 3" × 6" (8cm × 15cm) finished size Flying Geese Unit, cut a 3½" (9cm)-wide fabric strip. Feel familiar?

6. Cut triangles as shown, first placing the yellow cutting guideline along bottom edge of strip and then along top edge (Photo B). The yellow shaded area of the ruler will extend beyond the edge of the strip. That's where the magic of the ruler is… Note: Your triangles will be halfway pre-trimmed of the tiny fabric tips that you usually cut off after sewing! (These are called "dog-ears.")

7. Join half-square triangles to quar-ter-square triangle to complete 1 Flying Geese Unit (Photo C). HONK!

A

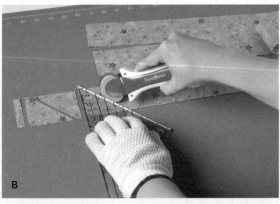

B

Video!
Flying Geese are made crystal clear in this video: **FonsandPorter. com/FlyingGeese**.

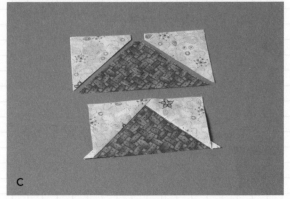

C

Kristi Loeffelholz

Kristi Loeffelholz serves as Group Publisher and Community Leader at Fons & Porter, overseeing titles such as *Quilty*, *Love of Quilting*, *Easy Quilts*, among many others.

What is the role of a publisher?
A publisher is responsible for leading the strategy and implementation of the content for a title like *Quilty*. I also work with F+W's executive team to develop, launch and grow brand extensions, new products and develop new markets for *Quilty*.

You believed in the *Quilty* mission from the start. How come?
I love the quilting industry. After being in the business for a decade, I was ready to do something about the gap in content for beginners. I loved the video aspect—most people (like me) look for a video to teach them something before they're confident enough to take a formal class. The market needed a point of entry and *Quilty* fit that mold well.

What does *Quilty* do well?
I am a big fan of *Quilty*, obviously, and feel *Quilty* does an excellent job of teaching the newbie quilter—and someone who has been quilting awhile—new skills. I love how the magazine ties in video for instruction; with the e-commerce portion, we complete "the loop" for our customer.

Where do you see *Quilty* in five years? Ten?
I would love to see *Quilty* continue to grow with the online show viewership at QNNtv.com, I would love to see magazine subscriptions launched (formal print and digital) and make it the largest-circulated quilting publication. I'd love to see brand extensions, such as *Quilty* classes online and at local shops, *Quilty* events, and possibly *Quilty* branded quilt kits. The sky is the limit!

A Quick Quilter's Glossary: More Words You Should Know

Here are a few more terms you can place squarely in your toolbox.

Autograph Quilt: Also called a "memory quilt" or a "signature quilt," this quilt offers spaces for signatures from friends, family, community, etc., usually for an important life event such as a wedding or graduation.

Backing: The back fabric of a quilt. See Quilt Sandwich.

Baste: To tack with long, loose stitches in preparation for sewing. Typically sewn by hand, basting stitches hold fabric layers or seams in place temporarily and are removed after final sewing. Basting with safety pins is a common practice for quilters preparing a "quilt sandwich."

Binding: The cloth that covers and protects the outer edges of a quilt.

Fat Quarter: A precut piece of fabric made by cutting a half yard in half again vertically. The resulting piece is approximately 18" × 22" (46cm × 56cm), which allows for cutting larger pieces than what a standard quarter yard would give you. (Standard ¼ yard [23cm] = 9" × 44" [23cm × 112cm])

Finished Size: The final sewn measurement of a completed block or quilt. Another way to say it: patchwork dimensions minus the seam allowances. So an 8" (20cm) finished measurement block would be cut 8½" (22cm) to allow for those ¼" (6mm) seam allowances.

Half-Square Triangle: A triangle made by cutting a square in half from corner to corner.

Quilt Guild: An association of quilters for mutual benefit and/or the pursuit of a common goal, often charitable in nature.

Quilt Sandwich, The: The three layers of a quilt: top, batting, backing.

Raw Edge: The non-serged, unstitched edge of a piece of fabric.

Seam Allowance: The width of fabric left to the right of a sewn seam. In quilting this is traditionally ¼" (6mm). For sewing garments it is usually ⅝" (16mm).

Triangle-squares: A square of patchwork made from two half-square triangles.

UFO: An "unfinished object." Slang.

Amelia

MATERIALS

3½ yards (3.2m) pink solid for sashing, borders, and binding

¾ yard (69cm) green solid for blocks

1 yard (91cm) black solid for blocks

¾ yard (69cm) blue solid for blocks

¾ yard (69cm) each of 6 assorted prints for blocks

Paper for foundation piecing

4½ yards (4.1m) backing fabric

Twin-size quilt batting

CUTTING

Measurements include seam allowances. Pieces for foundation piecing are cut oversize.

From pink solid, cut:
- 7 (3½" [9cm]-wide) strips. From strips, cut 35 (3½" × 7½" [9cm × 19cm]) vertical sashing rectangles.

- 8 (2¼" [6cm]-wide) strips for binding.

From remainder of pink solid, cut:
- 10 (3½" [9cm]-wide) lengthwise strips. From strips, cut 6 (3½" × 57½" [9cm × 146cm]) horizontal sashing rectangles, 2 (3½" × 67½" [9cm × 171cm]) side borders, and 2 (3½" × 63½" [9cm × 161cm]) top and bottom borders.

From your green solid, cut:
- 14 (3" × 5" [8cm × 13cm]) rectangles for foundation piecing (A1).

- 14 (2½" × 6½" [6cm × 17cm]) rectangles for foundation piecing (A6).

- 14 (2½" [6cm]) squares for foundation piecing (B1).

- 14 (1" × 5½" [3cm × 11cm]) rectangles for foundation piecing (A4).

- 14 (1" × 4½" [3cm × 11cm]) rectangles for foundation piecing (B4).

continued on next page

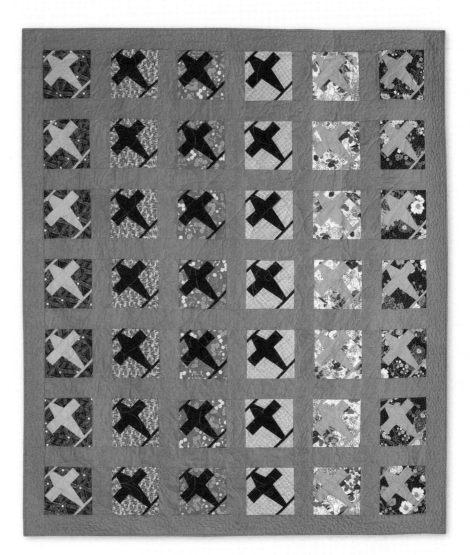

It's a bird! It's a plane! Okay, it's definitely a plane! Take flight with bold pink and a darling airplane block.

QUILT BY Quilty & Co.
QUILTED BY TailorMade by Design
63" × 73" (160cm × 185cm)
42 (7" [18cm]) blocks
Beginner Level 3

Editor's Note: This quilt was designed in-house after I spied an antique quilt with this unbelievable bubble-gum pink sashing and similar airplane blocks. It was a quilt that everyone loved and no one really knew what to do with, but *Quilty* welcomes those "orphans" as long as they have that special something. Amelia sure did—it was almost a cover quilt for us in 2013.

continued from previous page

From your black solid, cut:

- 21 (3" × 5" [8cm × 13cm]) rectangles for foundation piecing (A1).

- 21 (2½" × 6½" [6cm × 17cm]) rectangles for foundation piecing (A6).

- 21 (2½" [6cm]) squares for foundation piecing (B1).

- 21 (1" × 5½" [3cm × 14cm]) rectangles for foundation piecing (A4).

- 21 (1" × 4½" [3cm × 11cm]) rectangles for foundation piecing (B4).

From blue solid, cut:

- 7 (3" × 5" [8cm × 13cm]) rectangles for foundation piecing (A1).

- 7 (2½" × 6½" [6cm × 17cm]) rectangles for foundation piecing (A6).

- 7 (2½" [6cm]) squares for foundation piecing (B1).

- 7 (1" × 5½" [3cm × 14cm]) rectangles for foundation piecing (A4).

- 7 (1" × 4½" [3cm × 11cm]) rectangles for foundation piecing (B4).

From each ⅝ yard (57cm) piece, cut:

- 7 (4½" [11cm]) squares. Cut squares in half diagonally to make 14 half-square triangles for foundation piecing (A7 and A8).

- 4 (4" [10cm]) squares. Cut squares in half diagonally to make 7 half-square triangles for foundation piecing (A5).

- 14 (3½" × 4½" [9cm × 11cm]) rectangles for foundation piecing (A2 and A3).

- 14 (3½" × 2½" [9cm × 6cm]) rectangles for foundation piecing (B2 and B3).

- 4 (3" [8cm]) squares. Cut squares in half diagonally to make 7 half-square triangles for foundation piecing (B5).

Block Assembly

1. Photocopy 42 each of Foundation Units A and B from the patterns in the Templates section at the end of this book.

2. Referring to Block Unit Diagrams, paper piece foundation units in numerical order. Make 6 sets of 7 matching Unit A. Make 6 sets of 7 matching Unit B.

3. Lay out 1 Unit A and 1 matching Unit B as shown in Block Assembly Diagram. Join to complete 1 block (Block Diagram). Make 42 blocks.

Quilt Assembly

1. Lay out blocks and pink sashing rectangles as shown in Quilt Top Assembly Diagram.

2. Join into rows; join rows to complete quilt center.

3. Add side borders to quilt center. Add top and bottom borders to quilt.

Finishing

1. Divide backing into 2 (2¼-yard [2.1m]) lengths. Cut 1 piece in half to make 2 narrow panels. Join 1 narrow panel to each side of wider panel; press seam allowances toward narrow panels.

2. Layer backing, batting, and quilt top; baste. Quilt as desired. Quilt shown was quilted with an all over cloud design in quilt center and meandering in border (Quilting Diagram).

3. Join 2¼" (6cm)-wide pink strips into 1 continuous piece for straight-grain French-fold binding. Add binding to quilt. Fly into sky.

Video!
Marianne and Mary Fons want to help you make this block. Check out **HeyQuilty.com/Amelia** to watch this episode.

Unit A

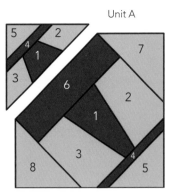

Block Unit Diagrams

Unit B

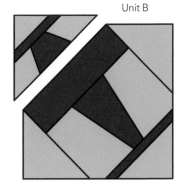

Block Assembly Diagram

Block Diagram

Fabric Note
Airplane blocks made with Art Gallery Prints.

We 🖤 this block!!

Tip Top Tip
For instructions and
a video on founda-
tion piecing, go to
**fonsandporter.com/
foundationpiecing.**

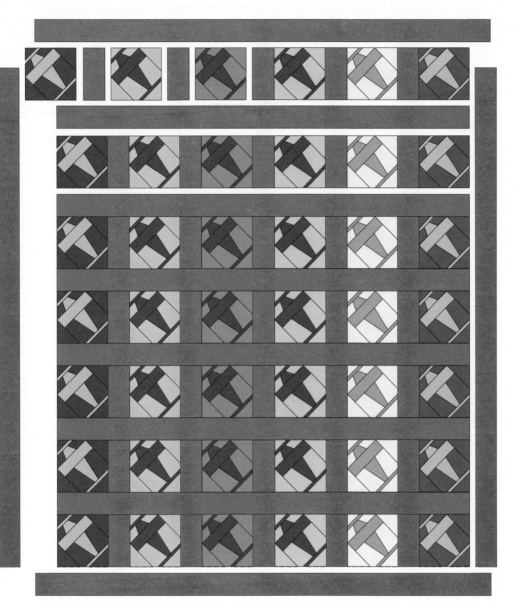

Quilt Top Assembly Diagram

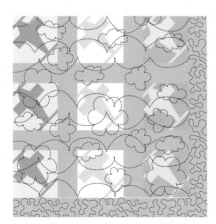

Quilting Diagram

Spooly Says

"This quilt was inspired by an antique Mary
saw. For incredible, instant inspiration, type
'antique quilts' into your browser, or visit an
exhibit or market featuring antique quilts."

11 Essential Tools for Quilters

1. **Sewing Machine.** We live in a world full of sewing machines that would make your great-grandmother weep with joy. *Quilty* highly recommends visiting a certified sewing machine dealer. Whether it's your first machine or your third, a dealer can answer questions, do repairs, and help "fit" you with one of the best friends you'll ever have.

2. **Fabric.** Cotton fabric is best: don't try to make a quilt out of grandma's hankies your first time out. A great quilt shop will help you find what you like and steer you away from inexpensive, flimsy fabrics and into the world of luxurious quilting-grade cotton.

3. **Rotary Cutter, Ruler, and Mat.** There are many ways to cut fabric, but the vast majority of quilters today use the rotary cutting system. The rotary cutter is essentially a razor blade on a wheel; the ruler (start with a 6" × 24" [15cm × 61cm]) offers an edge against which to cut; the mat (24" × 36" [61cm × 91cm] is best) protects your table and your blade. A quilt shop will have these items on hand and can help you understand how to use them safely.

4. **Iron and Ironing Board.** Making patchwork is three things: cutting, sewing, and pressing. Pressing your patchwork sets your seams and crisps up the units and blocks. Get a good iron and a safe pressing surface, and always unplug your iron when you're done.

5. **Seam Ripper.** Nobody's perfect.

6. **Design Wall.** A design wall is a place for your patchwork so you can see what's happening. A large piece of white flannel or thin quilt batting tacked up will do; there are also pre-made design walls available.

7. **Pins and Pincushion.** Thin, glass head pins are essential for basic patchwork. You'll be using them to hold units and rows in place.

8. **Scissors.** We really believe you need two kinds of scissors at your sewing table: a pair of large shears and a smaller pair of thread cutting/snipping scissors. When you get them, use them only for cutting fabric and thread.

9. **A Pattern.** Your pattern is your GPS, your quilt recipe. Find the one that speaks to you in a magazine, online, from a book, or a friend and refer to it often.

10. **Thread.** Thread comes in an endless number of colors a well as different weights, textures, and material types. For basic patchwork, look for a thread that reads 50/3 (this refers to the weight and yarn count) in the color of your choice.

11. **Time.** It's hard to make a quilt if you're not sewing. Make time for yourself and your hobby. Creative pursuits feed us in all kinds of ways; working on a quilt can actually make you feel like you have more time for everything else.

"Make It Your Own" + "Doodle Your Design Here"

BY MARY FONS

In the beginning, Mary drew all the MIYOs. Then we realized that computers draw better than Mary.

The question every more-seasoned quilter gets asked by beginners is probably: "Can you help me choose fabric?" While there are newbies who quickly take to selecting fabrics, there are more who have actual fear about the process: They're afraid they'll "mess up" their quilt before they've even begun.

Choosing the fabric for your quilt is hard, if you think about it. You've got value to consider, and contrast. You've got to find fabrics that "play well" together, that have "friends" and that don't "misbehave"—indeed, choosing fabric is a lot like roudning up a group of rowdy kindergartners.

The good news is that there's a straightforward way to figure out what fabrics should go into your quilt: play with them. Before you cut anything—even before you buy anything at the quilt shop—you can "audition" fabrics by placing them with each other, standing back, and seeing what you think. When you see a quilt in the pages of *Quilty* that you want to make, you can take the pattern to the quilt shop and "audition" this fabric with that one and get a selection that you think will work. You can also get out a colored pencil set, if you're just looking to explore color combinations, and doodle a bit.

The MIYO doodles that run with every quilt pattern are there to get the audition process started. Is the quilt in the magazine made in pinks and blues? The MIYOs show you a block from the quilt in greens and yellows, perhaps, just to help you visualize how you can—wait for it—make that quilt your own. Because when you skip the kit and change the color scheme with your own fabric choices, you have really created something original—and that's the ticket to happy, rewarding quiltmaking for a lifetime.

Around the end of 2013, we introduced the "Doodle your own quilting design here" concept in the Quilting Diagram sections. This is a second Quilting Diagram image with no marks on it at all so that readers can get out a pen and doodle some motifs for themselves.

The idea helps people see that a) the quilting shown in the pattern is truly just a suggestion; and b) the creative process includes the quilting of your quilt. We heard feedback quickly that the "create your own" space was appreciated and so far, *Quilty* seems to be the only quilt magazine with such a feature.

August Intensity

MATERIALS

3–4 fat quarters* assorted yellow-green fabrics and gold-green fabrics

7–8 fat quarters* assorted medium rust fabrics and red fabrics

5 fat quarters* assorted dark purple, blue, and red fabrics

½ yard (46cm) dark purple fabric for binding

3½ yards (3.2m) backing fabric

Twin-size quilt batting

*Fat quarter = 18" × 20" (46cm × 51cm)

CUTTING

Measurements include ¼" (6mm) seam allowances.

From assorted yellow-green solids and gold-green fabrics, cut:
- 9 (6" [15cm]-wide) strips. From strips, cut a total of 27 (6" [15cm]) squares.

From assorted medium rust solids and red fabrics, cut:
- 21 (6" [15cm]-wide) strips. From strips, cut a total of 63 (6" [15cm]) squares.

From assorted dark purple, blue, and red fabrics, cut:
- 14 (6" [15cm]-wide) strips. From strips, cut a total of 40 (6" [15cm]) squares.

From dark purple fabric, cut:
- 7 (2¼" [6mm]-wide) strips for binding.

Fabric Note
Fabrics are from the Jason Yenter Modern Solids collection from In The Beginning.

Gross outside? Here's a juicy slice of summer. Easiest quilt ever.

QUILT BY Emily Blatt
55" × 71½" (140cm × 182cm)
Beginner Level 1

Editor's Note: This quilt makes use of analogous colors, which is a fancy way to say "colors close together on the color wheel." But however you describe it technically, Emily made a modern quilt here, using values of reds, magentas, ambers, and burnt oranges to convey the warmth of summer itself. Simple squares, perfectly placed.

Quilt Assembly

1. Lay out squares as shown in Quilt Top Assembly Diagram. Join squares into rows; join rows to complete quilt center.

Finishing

1. Divide backing into 2 (1¾-yard [1.6m]) lengths. Join pieces lengthwise. Seam will run horizontally.

2. Layer backing, batting, and quilt top; baste. Quilt as desired. Quilt shown was quilted with a meandering scroll design.

3. Join 2¼" (6cm)-wide dark purple strips into 1 continuous piece for straight-grain French-fold binding. Add binding to quilt.

Designer Profile

Emily Blatt learned to sew in 7th grade Home Economics class, and learned to quilt in 2009. She has always made things but, for now, she concentrates on quilting and knitting. Emily is a member of the Boston Modern Quilt Guild. In her spare time, she works in health care finance at a hospital in New Hampshire.

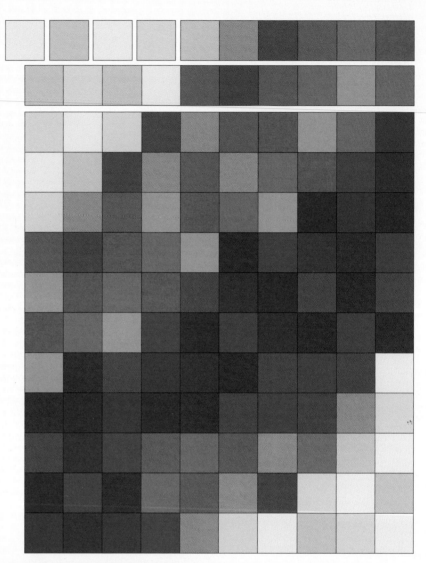

Quilt Top Assembly Diagram

Make It Your Own

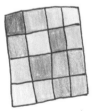

Sherwood Forest

Neutral middle, pink hues...nice!

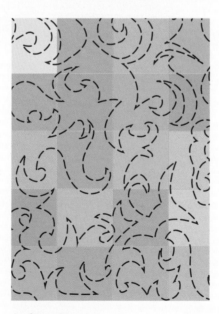

Quilting Diagram

Spooly Says

"Reading glasses will protect your eyes at the sewing machine. As if you needed an excuse for fashion."

Safe Rotary Cutting

Introduced in the 1980s, the rotary cutter revolutionized the way we make quilts. Essentially a razor blade on a wheel, the rotary cutter slices through fabric like a hot knife through butter. But with rotary cutting power comes great responsibility.

Video!
We capture a quilter using a rotary cutter for the first time!
HeyQuilty.com/Rotary

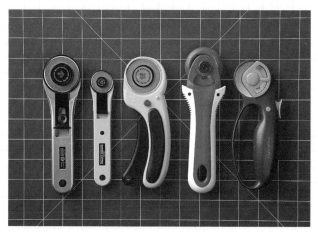

1. Make sure you have the right tool for the job. If you're cutting small circles, you'll want a small rotary cutter. Larger strips? Go bigger.

Bad   Good

2. Change your blade when it gets dull. How often you change your blade depends on how much fabric you're cutting. Cutting a lot? Change your blade every couple of weeks. Use it rarely? Maybe mark the back of your cutter with a piece of masking tape that tells you when you last changed the blade. Just as a dull kitchen knife is potentially more dangerous than a sharp one, so it is with a dull rotary blade—you have to exert more pressure to get a clean cut.

3. Always, always close your blade!

Practice with your cutter so you know the "open" and "close" positions.

4. Always cut away from yourself, never toward yourself.

5. Use a safety glove for extra protection.

Colorful Chevrons

MATERIALS

14 fat quarters* assorted bright solids for blocks

3½ yards (3.2m) navy solid for blocks and binding

Fons & Porter Quarter Inch Seam Marker (optional)

4½ yards (4.1m) backing fabric

Twin-size quilt batting

*Fat quarter = 18" × 20" (46cm × 51cm)

CUTTING

Measurements include ¼" (6mm) seam allowances.

From fat quarters, cut a total of:
- 40 (4⅞" [12cm]-wide) strips. From strips, cut 160 (4⅞" [12cm]) squares.

From navy solid, cut:
- 20 (4⅞" [12cm]-wide) strips. From strips, cut 160 (4⅞" [12cm]) squares.
- 8 (2¼" [6cm]-wide) strips for binding.

Fabric Note
Fabrics are from Michael Miller.

Color in yo' FACE.

QUILT BY Christa Watson
64" × 80" (163cm × 203cm)
80 (8" [20cm]) blocks
Beginner Level 1

Editor's Note: I'm not sure when it happened, but chevrons took over the quilting world at some point. They were printed on fabric, created with patchwork, and generally made it onto anything that could be sewn with a needle and thread. And why not? The chevron is a great motif, and Christa's quilt interpreted the mighty chevron in a way that *Quilty* felt was fresh and downright irresistible. A cover quilt for us for the Nov/Dec '13 issue.

Block Assembly

1. Referring to Triangle-Square Diagram, place Quarter Inch Seam Marker diagonally across wrong side of 1 bright square, with yellow center line positioned exactly at corners. Mark stitching guidelines along both sides of Quarter Inch Seam Marker.

2. Place square atop 1 navy square, right sides facing; stitch along marked sewing lines. Cut between rows of stitching to make 2 triangle-squares. Make 320 triangle-squares.

3. Lay out 2 pairs of matching triangle-squares as shown in the Block Assembly Diagram. Join the triangle-squares into rows; join the rows to complete 1 block (Block Diagram). Make 80 blocks.

Quilt Assembly

1. Lay out blocks as shown in Quilt Top Assembly Diagram.

2. Join blocks into rows; join rows to complete quilt top.

Finishing

1. Divide backing into 2 (2¼-yard [2.1m]) lengths. Join panels length-wise.

2. Layer backing, batting, and quilt top; baste. Quilt as desired. Quilt shown was quilted with straight lines in the bright triangles, and with straight lines and a circle design in the navy background (Quilting Diagram).

3. Join 2¼" (6cm)-wide navy strips into 1 continuous piece for straight-grain French-fold binding. Add binding to quilt.

Designer Profile

Christa Watson loves to inspire others to make their own quilts and have fun doing it. She enjoys life with her hubby and 3 kids in Las Vegas where she blogs about quilting, sells fabric online, and sneaks in as much quilting time as she can. You can visit Christa at ChristaQuilts.com.

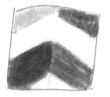

Make It Your Own

Lighten it up with white instead of navy?

 Note
If you are not using the Fons & Porter Quarter Inch Seam Marker, draw a diagonal line from corner to corner across square. Then draw sewing lines on each side of the first line, ¼" (6mm) away.

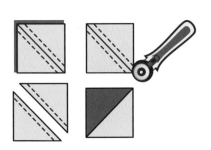

Triangle-Square Diagram

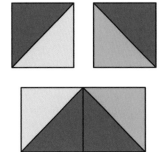

Block Assembly Diagram

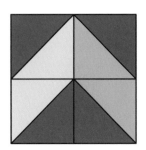

Block Diagram

Quilt Top Assembly Diagram

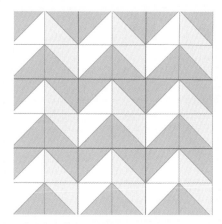

Doodle your own quilting design here.

Quilting Diagram

Cutting Half-Square Triangles

Spooly Says

"With this ruler, you can cut HSTs and QSTs. Make sure you're using the 'yellow' side this time."

With a Fons & Porter Half and Quarter Ruler, you can easily cut half-square triangles from strips. How cool is that?

1. Straighten the left edge of fabric strip. Place the line of the Fons & Porter Half and Quarter Ruler that corresponds with your strip width on the bottom edge of strip, aligning left edge of ruler with straightened edge of strip. The yellow tip of ruler will extend beyond top edge of strip.

2. Cut along right edge of ruler to make 1 half-square triangle (Photo A).

3. Turn ruler and align same line with top edge of strip. Now, the little yellow nib will hang below the bottom edge of the strip. Cut along right edge of ruler (Photo B).

4. Repeat to cut required number of half-square triangles.

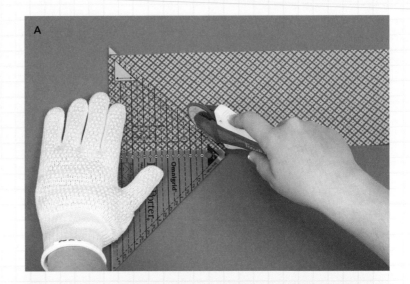

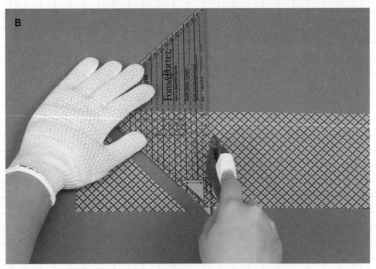

You will get the hang of it and then you will love this method!

Watch the tool in action on this episode of *Quilty*: **HeyQuilty. com/HalfQuarterRuler.**

Jack Newell and Rebecca Fons

Rebecca Fons and Jack Newell, 2014. The heart and soul of *Quilty*, respectively.

Jack Newell, director, and Rebecca Fons, producer, have been on Team Quilty since the very first episode in 2011. Jack is an award-winning filmmaker who works professionally in the film and television industry; Rebecca has served as the Education Program Manager of the Chicago International Film Festival since 2009 and has many production credits to her name, as well. They both live in Chicago where *Quilty* is taped twice a year.

MARY: Jack, what, if anything, do quilters and filmmakers have in common?

JACK: I think both strive for perfection, which is maybe impossible, but we share a desire to make something perfect. Acknowledging details is super important, because a quilt is made up of a lot of small details. If you screw up a lot of those details, you miss the boat, and making films is similar. Quilters have a pattern they're going off of, filmmakers use a script. We can also take mistakes and make them into opportunities. Also, like filmmakers, quilters love snacks and finger foods.

MARY: You make feature-length films, documentaries, commercials, etc. How is making a how-to show different from projects where you're telling a narrative story?

JACK: When we started the show many years ago, it was a great opportunity, just from a business standpoint. But it also presented a great challenge for me artistically because as it turns out, [making an episode] is telling a story. Now, *Quilty* isn't The Odyssey.

But it is a story, and there's a problem that needs to be solved. You can roll your eyes at how-to shows, and people do, but they are interesting and there's something important that needs to happen, which is the learning objective, but the show also needs to be entertaining, interesting, fun, engaging -- all those words. And you have to tell a story. By the end of the episode, if you haven't told the story, you've failed.

MARY: Rebecca, tell me about working with your mom and your sister.

REBECCA: Something I learned really quickly is that when you work with your family, when you have a job you have to get done, the grudges you have—your sister stole your hairbrush when you were younger, or whatever—none of those petty squabbles should come into play. That doesn't mean they don't always, but you just have to get over it. You, Mary, have to answer to me sometimes and I have to do your bidding at times. Those can be pride-swallowing moments but I have to take my sister hat off and put on my producer hat and focus on the job at hand.

And don't forget, I work with my soon-to-be husband, too. It's like the Island of Misfit Toys, sometimes!

JACK: But it's fun.

REBECCA: And working with Mom is always great because like… She is "Marianne Fons" to all these people… but she's just "Mom" to me, so when I see her work, I get the biggest kick out of it. I don't mean that condecendingly. I love to watch her work because I see so clearly why everybody loves her. She's great.

JACK: She's really good.

REBECCA: She'll just be Mom and then the camera goes on, but...she's the same. She's just so genuine. It's great to see how genuine she is and to know that her success is based on the fact that she's incredibly talented and incredibly genuine. And that is such an honest way to make a living. I really admire that. It's made me admire her in a whole new way. I just think she's the tops. And it's great she gives you space Mary, to create your own thing. She's always a complement. We're always excited to see Mom on the show. And the crew shapes up when she's around.

MARY: Tell me about a "most memorable moment."

REBECCA: I have two. One is when I insisted we do the Helmet Cam. I was adamant that we do it and no one else wanted to do it. But I was like, "I've got a helmet, we've got a Go-Pro [portable mini-digital camera]. We're gonna put the Go-Pro on the helmet, and Mary's gonna film her P.O.V. from the Quilty Cam. And you guys were like, "Whatever, okay." And then I did actually bring everything and said, "We're gonna do it, right?" And you guys did it. Jack like, adorably taped the camera to the helmet and Mary, you had to sit real funny. But I was just... I was so happy that we did it. We never did it again, so clearly it wasn't a winner. It was just fun to have a funny idea and be supported in that idea.

I also will never forget when you lost it and starting laughing so hard talking about... What was it? Goose foot? Baby quilts or something??

MARY: The "fifty babies" thing! [Episode 215, "How to Have a Strip-Swap-Cutting-Bee-Fabric Exchange Party!]

REBECCA: We kept it in the episode because talk about genuine! That was such a genuine "you" moment that articulated how much fun you were having.

MARY: Some people didn't like it.

REBECCA: I saw that! Some people commented on that episode and said stuff like, "get it together!" But we were having so much fun and that's part of Quilty, to show how much fun it is to create and to be creative and to be an artist. And sometimes that means you get the giggles. So we kept it in because it showed a side of Quilty that's a very real side. And why shouldn't we, in a measured way, show that? From the moment you started getting the giggles to seeing it in the episode, I thought that was really fun.

JACK: I remember that first shoot. The first four episodes we shot in the old Quiltology space on Halsted.

REBECCA: We loaded in at five in the morning.

JACK: We did?

REBECCA: Yeah. It was dark when we loaded in. It was in August. During the Air and Water show.

JACK: Wasn't it dark when we left, too?

MARY: Yeah. Gosh, those first shows were so hard.

JACK: Did we really take two full days to shoot four episodes? It's possible.

MARY: We had to turn the air conditioner off for sound quality. It was so hot under the lights. That was tough.

REBECCA: I just thought of an ongoing "favorite memory." On the set, in between takes, everyone will talk about our lives, culture, everything, really. Sometimes things get a little bawdy. We're on a ship and it's like... the poop deck. There are a lot of inside jokes. If there is any joke to be made about quilting, we've made it. Good naturedly, of course.

MARY: You two are getting married soon. You know you're probably going to get a wedding quilt, right? Any color preferences or patterns you'd like to request?

JACK: Who's asking? [laughs]

REBECCA: The person who would be putting the quilt together knows us, so we'd want the quilter to make those choices. It'll be a more special quilt if it's a total surprise.

MARY: Can we feature the quilt on Quilty?

REBECCA: Absolutely!

MARY: Would that be the first time Jack Newell would be on Quilty, then? [Jack, despite years of our begging, steadfastly refuses to be on camera.]

JACK: No.

REBECCA: It's so annoying that you'll never be on Quilty. What if we wrapped you up in the quilt and we just put you in the background? Like a quilt burrito.

JACK: Well, I need to do work on the other side. Rebecca's job is to produce, so on set, she's more in a position to be on camera; she also has more knowledge. I don't know how you do it, Mary. The on-camera stuff. I would not want to be a host on a television show. It's so hard. I've been on camera before, but it's acting, it's not being yourself. It's a challenge. I'd rather not do that. I like being behind the camera.

MARY: Rebecca, do you like being on the show? People really like you on the show.

REBECCA: I love being on the show. Especially being on a "This Is My Quilt" episode, which I've done several times because I have so many quilts. I like doing those shows because I like talking to you, Mary, and I love the quilts that I have. And I thoroughly enjoyed being the Quilt Police

[*Quilty* episode 242, "What Is the Quilt Police?"]. I feel, perhaps, the Police may be "on the beat soon." Some tickets are due, probably. I certainly would not object to that.

MARY: What's the hardest part of making *Quilty*?

REBECCA: The *Quilty* set is a blank slate and we make it every time. We create that set, soup to nuts, every time we shoot. We have been able to design the look and you've been able to direct that, and we make it unique and cozy. But it's not like the lights turn off on the *Quilty* set and we lock the door with an adorable key and then next time, it's like, "Hi!" No, we open boxes, put it all back together.

JACK: It's labor intensive.

REBECCA: Coordination is tough. We film twice a year and at this point, we're really good at making the show, but that first episode or so, our muscles are like, tight. We have to wake up that part of us that knows how to do it.

JACK: The first episode after lunch is always really hard. Because I'm really tired.

REBECCA: Yeah, and morning call time is at 7:00AM. That stinks.

MARY: How about the best part?

REBECCA: The best is cast and crew! We have so much fun. Everyone is really good at what they do. We're super respectful of our time and professional about our schedule; we keep our eyes on the prize. Everybody congratulates and pats each other on the back, after each episode, after each day, and after each show,. I think guests feel that right away. And viewers feel that.

Oh, plus, we film the show in a loft in Pilsen and there's a cat on set. So that's pretty cool.

Good morning!

I guess you would call me a newbie, but since my background is in the arts, I would describe myself as a confident beginner. I love *Quilty*!

The magazine is a great mix of traditional and modern quilt-making—really a great balance. The *Quilty* videos help to clarify technique and have encouraged me to buy many Fons & Porter products. (That should please the folks in marketing and sales!)

One item that is not available through the web store is a *Quilty* mug. Do you have any plans to sell these or other items with the *Quilty* logo? I would love to have a mug in my sewing space because your magazine/show continues to inspire my creativity.

Thanks so much for the inspiration!

Daphne Demopulos
Sent from my iPad

Many fine products—maybe even mugs—are available at the *Quilty* online store.

Sunny Side Up

MATERIALS

1¾ yards (1.6m) of yellow solid for blocks

6¼ yards (5.7m) of white solid for blocks, sashing, border, and binding

6 yards (5.5m) of backing fabric

Full-size quilt batting

CUTTING

Measurements include ¼" (6mm) seam allowances. Patterns for A and B are in the Templates section at the end of this book. Border strips are exact length needed. You may want to cut them longer to allow for piecing variations.

From yellow solid, cut:
- 96 B.

From white, cut:
- 3 (9" [23cm]-wide) strips. From strips, cut 12 (9" [23cm]) D squares.

- 8 (6½" [17cm]-wide) strips. Piece strips to make 2 (6½" × 81¼"[17cm × 206cm]) side borders and 2 (6½" × 72" [17cm × 183cm]) top and bottom borders.

- 15 (4¾" [12cm]-wide) strips. From 10 strips, cut 8 (4¾" × 17½" [12cm × 44cm]) E rectangles and 48 (4¾" [12cm]) C squares. Piece remaining strips to make 3 (4¾" × 60" [12cm × 152cm]) F sashing strips.

- 9 (2¼" [6cm]-wide) strips for binding.

- 96 A.

Fabric Note
Fabrics are from Kaufman Essex Linen in Sunshine Yellow & Michael Miller Cotton Couture in Solid White.

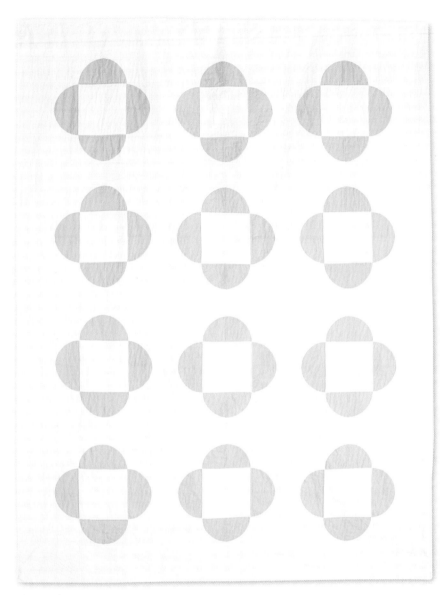

So, so happy.

QUILT BY Anna Graham
71½" × 92¾" (182cm ×236cm)
12 (17" [43cm]) blocks
Beginner Level 3

Editor's Note: Sunshine? Breakfast? Yellow flowers? However you interpret the shapes and colors of this quilt, it evokes pure happiness. Curved seams scare a lot of beginners because they can take time to get the hang of. But though *Quilty* quilts are chosen for beginners, we believe in the abilities of our readers to take on a challenge. Besides, when the quilt at the end of the learning "curve" is as great as this one, the process is a pleasure.

Block Assembly

1. Join 1 white A and 1 yellow B as shown in Block Unit Diagrams. Make 96 Block Units.

2. Lay out 4 Block Units, 4 white C squares, and 1 white D square as shown in Block Assembly Diagram. Join into sections; join sections to complete 1 block (Block Diagram). Make 12 blocks.

Quilt Assembly

1. Lay out blocks, white E rectangles, and white F sashing strips as shown in Quilt Top Assembly Diagram.

2. Join into rows; join rows to complete quilt center.

3. Add white side borders to quilt center. Add white top and bottom borders to quilt.

Finishing

1. Divide backing into 2 (3-yard [2.75m]) lengths. Join panels lengthwise.

2. Layer backing, batting, and quilt top; baste. Quilt as desired. Quilt shown was quilted with straight lines (Quilting Diagram).

3. Join 2¼" (6cm)-wide white strips into 1 continuous piece for straight-grain French-fold binding. Add binding to quilt.

Designer Profile

Anna is a mom to two crazy but incredibly inspiring little girls (my noodleheads). She loves to sew and be creative. Anna grew up sewing with her mom and while it definitely wasn't her favorite thing to do, she loved being inspired to make something of her own. Having two daughters gave Anna the drive to start sewing more and after discovering the blogging world, she never turned back. Anna is having fun creating, making up new things as she goes along, discovering new techniques and making her house a home. You can learn more about Anna at Noodle-Head.com.

Make It Your Own

Add a yolk!

Or just pick your favorite color.

This is also a Pie 'N Crust block; we show you how on *Quilty!* **Hey-Quilty.com/PieNCrust**

Spooly Says

"Nice, sharp pins are crucial to nailing those curved seams. Take small bites with your pin, and don't be afraid to use a bunch!"

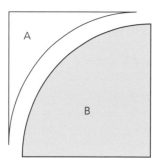

Block Unit Diagrams

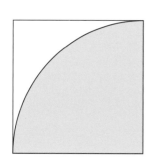

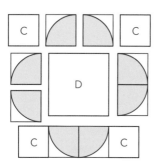

Block Assembly Diagram

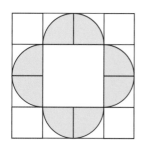

Block Diagram

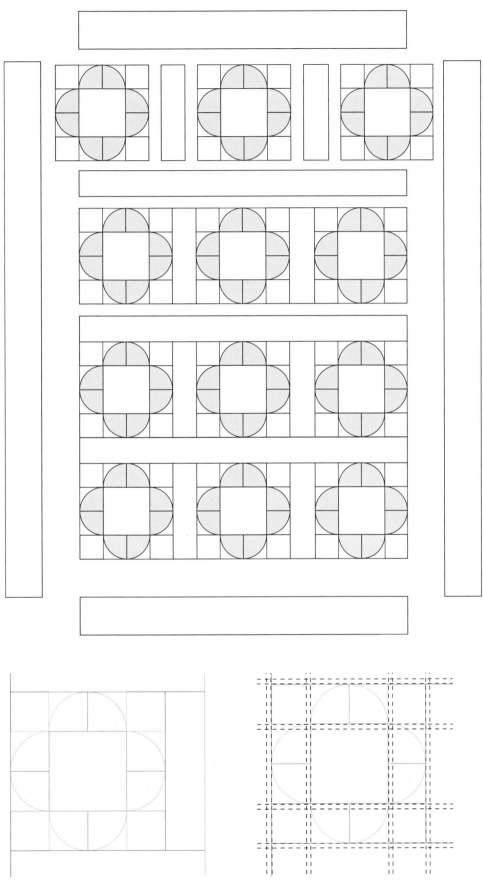

Doodle your own quilting design here.

Quilting Diagram

Sewing Curved Seams

When you're making any quilt with curved pieces, use these tips to sew curved seams more easily. It's all about the fluff.

1. After cutting the background "crust" and the quarter-circle "pie" pieces, mark the center of the curve on both pieces by folding each in half and creasing or making a small clip (Photo A).

2. Working with the background "crust" on top, place fabric right sides together. Then pin pieces together at curve centers, taking a small bite. At the end of the seam, align pieces and pin, taking a large bite (Photo B).

3. When you're ready to sew, make sure your pieces are lined up nicely. Stitch only to the middle of the curve. Use your fingertips to keep curved edges aligned or control the top fabric and keep edges aligned with a wooden skewer or stiletto (Photo C). Practice will help—don't worry if you mess up a few at first.

4. Leaving the needle in the fabric, raise the presser foot. "Fluff" the top "crust" fabric back toward where you have sewn (Photo D).

5. Align curved edges for the second half of the seam and stitch to about 1" (3cm) from end of seam. Stop again and "fluff" the top fabric so ending edges are also aligned. Sew to the end of the seam.

6. Gently press seam allowance toward background "crust" piece. Now try another "slice"!

We have a great *Quilty* episode on this. Check it out!
HeyQuilty.com/CurvedSeams

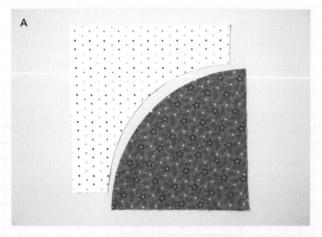

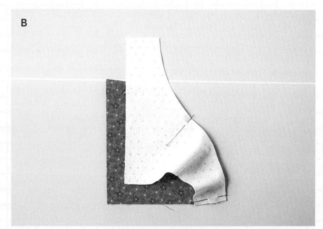

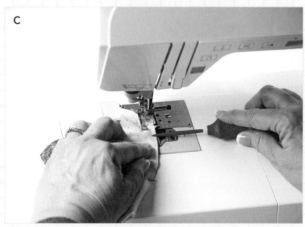

This Is My Quilt

BY MARY FONS

If you only ever saw quilts in quilt magazines, you'd think every quilt was perfect. Perfectly designed, perfectly executed, and done fast, too—there are countless quilts in a continual stream of quilt magazines and they all look, well...fancy.

This high standard is a good thing. People want to see the best of the best in quilt magazines; in order to teach techniques and best practicies, editoral teams want the best quilts, too. At Fons & Porter, we run quilts with top-notch workmanship, quilts that are design slam-dunks—even if you don't happen to like a particular quilt's style—and yes, they come in under deadline. Usually.

But the "perfect" quilts only tell a tiny portion of the story of quilts in our lives. What about all those imperfect quilts? The ones that would never land a page in a magazine in a million years? We love those quilts, too, right?

Wrong: We may love them more. In magazines, there are no batting lumps or binding bumps, not a single hint that a baby, a dog, or a cat has been anywhere near the quilt, ever. But we know the truth about the quilts in our lives. Why shouldn't we publicly celebrate those quilts, too?

When the show started, I wanted to have a "quilt show" segment that would recur. People (quilters as well as non-quilters) love to see quilts and hear their story. The best stories are usually about the quilts that have stains on them. "This Is My Quilt" was born out of the desire to hear those great stories and celebrate the imperfections in the quilts in our lives. At last, the non-perfect quilt could get its place in the sun.

Since 2011, we've filmed dozens of "This Is My Quilt" segments. We've had a doggie quilt, a memory quilt, a fan-girl quilt for a video game character, an art quilt found in an antique store, a "first-time making a [fill-in-the-blank] quilt," a graduation quilt, a quilt that hasn't been finished, a threadbare quilt, and many more. With the quilt comes the owner, who shares with the *Quilty* viewers the "scoop."

The magazine feature that goes along with the episode is sort of a continuation of the interview and an opportunity to go deeper as well as bring that particular quilt to a larger audience. Someone who has never seen *Quilty* the show might pick up the magazine at their LQS or bookstore and read about the featured "TIMQ." Then they go to the web, see the quilt, and that quilt gets to live a little longer, with a little more glory.

Jack and Matt H. hang a quilt for a TIMQ episode.

Modern Pinwheels

MATERIALS

20 fat quarters* of assorted prints for blocks and binding

2⅜ yards (2.2m) cream solid for blocks

8½" (22cm) square ruler or template plastic

4 yards (3.7m) backing fabric

Twin-size quilt batting

*Fat quarter = 18" × 20" (46cm × 51cm)

CUTTING

Measurements include ¼" (6mm) seam allowances.

From each print fat quarter, cut:
- 4 (3½" [9cm]-wide) strips. From strips, cut 12 (3½" × 6½" [9cm × 17cm]) B rectangles.

- 1 (2¼" [6cm]) strip for binding.

From cream solid, cut:
- 22 (3½" [9cm]) strips. From strips, cut 236 (3½" [9cm]) A squares.

Fabric Note
Jay used fabrics from his Center City line for Westminster.

A chic quilt from *Project Runway* winner and textile designer Jay McCarroll.

QUILT DESIGN BY Jay McCarroll
QUILT MADE AND MACHINE QUILTED BY Janet McCarroll
56" × 62½" (142cm × 159cm)
59 (8" [20cm]) blocks
Beginner Level 3

Editor's Note: I met Jay McCarroll (fabric and fashion designer, first-ever Project Runway winner) at the Quilters Take Manhattan event in New York City in 2011 and liked him right away. *Quilty* was just a show at that point, but there was discussion about the magazine, and I knew Jay would be one of the first designers I tapped if the magazine became a reality. He and his sister collaborated on this quilt expressly for *Quilty* and I was really grateful: we had scored a celebrity designer and a great, modern quilt.

BACK STORY

Janet talks back!

"I always do something 'piecey' on the backs of quilts I make. It just makes them more intriguing. The origin of a pieced back is simply an effort to utilize blocks that got rejected for the front as well as scraps from the making of the top. If one doesn't use 'rejected' blocks on the back, they languish in a closet. Many quilters tuck little scraps of fabric into the folded cuts leftover in their stash when a project is done. I do too, but it makes me batty. So, I opened up all of the folded fabrics from Jay's current and past fabric lines and used all of those (annoying) small remnants. It's a way of tidying up the fabric piles. For Pinwheel, I also threw in a few star blocks that were not used in a different quilt.

I love the process of randomly joining patches together and seeing what direction the backing takes. It's complete serendipity. It's liberating to have no rules after having to follow piecing rules for the front of a quilt. This is the most intricately pieced and time-consuming back I have ever done. I didn't set out for it to be that way, I just wasn't thinking properly!"

Block Assembly

1. Lay out 4 cream A squares and 4 matching print B rectangles as shown in Block Unit Assembly Diagram. Join each A and B as shown, then join 4 A/B sets.

2. Make a total of 59 Block Units.

3. Trim block units as shown in Trimming Diagram using an 8½" (22cm) square ruler or template plastic to complete block (Block Diagram).

Quilt Assembly

1. Lay out blocks in vertical rows as shown in Quilt Top Assembly Diagram. Lay out 4 rows of 8 blocks and 3 rows of 9 blocks. Join your blocks into rows.

2. Beginning with an 8-block row, stagger rows as shown in Quilt Top Assembly Diagram, matching cream triangles between rows so they make squares. Join rows.

3. Trim top and bottom edges of quilt center even with shortest row as shown.

Finishing

1. Divide backing into 2 (2-yard [1.8m]) lengths. Cut 1 piece in half lengthwise to make 2 narrow panels. Join 1 narrow panel to each side of wider panel; press seam allowances toward narrow panels.

2. Layer backing, batting, and quilt top; baste. Quilt as desired. Quilt shown was quilted with a meandering triangle design (Quilting Diagram).

3. Join 2¼" (6cm)-wide print strips into 1 continuous piece for straight-grain French-fold binding. Add binding to quilt. Looking good!

Video!

We show you how to bind your quilts in this super easy video: HeyQuilty.com/binding.

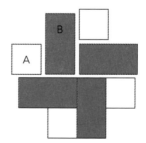

Block Unit Assembly Diagram

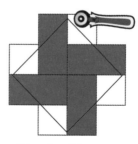

Trimming Diagram

Block Diagram

Designer Profile

Jay McCarroll won the inaugural season of the television show, *Project Runway*. Fabric, color, pattern, and texture are among the great loves of Jay's life. Manipulating those elements into functioning products for people to use and enjoy is the greatest part of his job. Learn more and shop at JayMccarrollonline.com.

Rich in solids

Experiment with isolating pinwheels.

Make It Your Own

Quilt Top Assembly Diagram

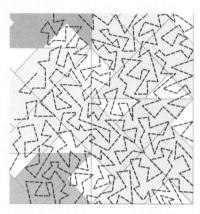

Quilting Diagram

Video!
Check out more pinwheel action: Vintage Fons & Porter!! **HeyQuilty.com/ oldschoolpinwheels**

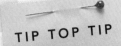

Auditioning a Quilt Design

Before you take the quilting leap on your sandwich, try out a few options with this handy method.

1. Get some Press 'n Seal plastic wrap at the store—you may have some in your pantry already! Note: This is not cling wrap or regular plastic wrap. That will make you cry. Make sure it's the new-fangled Press 'n Seal. Also obtain a wet erase marker, blue or black—dry erase markers leave "dust" (Photo A).

2. Tear out a sheet of the wrap and place it on your quilt. Using your marker, play around (Photos B and C)!

3. You have a few options. You can actually sew through the wrap and tear it off later, or just put the design you're happy with up on your design wall and refer to it as your guide as you quilt (Photos D and E).

A

B

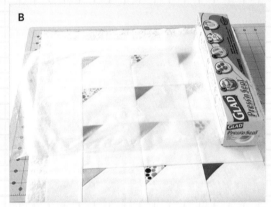

C

D

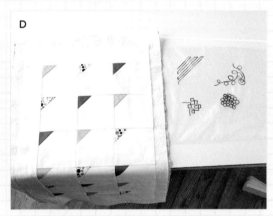

E

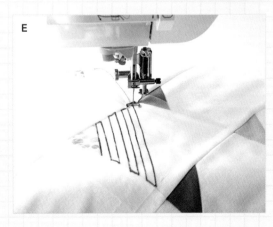

 Let Mary and Ebony take you through it: **HeyQuilty. com/QuiltDesign**

Alex Jones

Quilty set. Not pictured: Alex Jones.

Alex Jones is a film editor living in Los Angeles.

What do you do to make *Quilty*?
I provide the motion graphics and do some editing for *Quilty*, which means I make all of the titles and write out all of the tips. I've done it since the first show.

It's so crazy that you work in L.A., so far from the rest of the production. Do you feel like part of the team?
I've been involved since *Quilty* first started and I helped with the initial creation of the look and style of the titles, so I feel like I'm part of the core team.

At this point, if you had supplies and a copy of *Quilty*, do you think you could you make a quilt?
Yes! I think it helps that I have a bit of sewing experience already. But given the tools, I could do a pretty bang-up quilt.

How is editing a how-to show different from the other work you do, editing music videos and commercials?
The main difference in editing a series like this is showing enough coverage. Film and commercials are more forgiving because people aren't watching the editing too closely. But here, if you miss adding one close-up, it can completely throw someone off. They'll be like, "Whoa, how did she go from having a whole bunch of scraps on the table to a fully completed quilt!?" It requires a bit more thought about what needs to be shown to make it comprehensive.

What's the best part of the job?
The best part is seeing an episode come together. It comes in as a bunch of shots but eventually gets molded into a full episode, complete with titles and graphics. There's a real sense of accomplishment.

Mod Shape

MATERIALS

3 yards (2.75m) turquoise solid for blocks and binding

4 yards (3.7m) white solid for blocks and appliqué

1½ yards (1.4m) turquoise print for appliqué

1 fat quarter* orange solid for appliqué

Paper-backed fusible web

5 yards (4.6m) backing fabric

Twin-size quilt batting

*Fat quarter = 18" × 20" (46cm × 51cm)

CUTTING

Measurements include ¼" (6mm) seam allowances. Pattern for Petal is in the Templates section at the back of this book. Follow manufacturer's instructions for fusible web.

From turquoise solid, cut:
• 5 (16½" [42cm]-wide) strips. From strips, cut 10 (16½" [42cm]) squares.

• 8 (2¼" [6cm]-wide) strips for binding.

From white solid, cut:
• 5 (16½" [42cm]-wide) strips. From strips, cut 10 (16½" [42cm]) squares.

• 40 Petals.

From turquoise print, cut:
• 36 Petals.

From orange solid, cut:
• 4 Petals.

Fabric Note
Jenifer used a Stitch Square Palette print from the Mod Basics collection by Michael Miller, and solids by Michael Miller Fabrics.

Further proof that quilts are cool.

QUILT BY Jenifer Dick
QUILTED BY Kris Barlow
64" × 80" (163cm × 203cm)
20 (16" [41cm]) blocks
Beginner Level 2

- -

Editor's Note: This quilt just seems like it's floating in air—the style shot captured the feeling perfectly, and it ended up making the cover. This is a quilt that offers a challenge for a beginner, but we couldn't pass it up. A perfect blend of traditional and modern, Mod Shape shows just what a quilt in the 21st century can be: fun, unexpected, "clean," and classy.

Block Assembly

1. Referring to Block Assembly Diagram, fold 1 turquoise square in half diagonally in both directions; finger press. Position 4 white Petals atop turquoise square, matching petal tips with creases and leaving ¼" (6mm) space between petals; fuse in place.

2. Machine appliqué Petals to turquoise square as shown in Block Diagrams, using invisible thread and a zigzag stitch. Make 10 turquoise blocks.

3. In the same manner, make 9 white blocks using white squares and turquoise Petals.

4. Make 1 white block using remaining white square and 4 orange Petals.

Video!
For help on doing appliqué, check out a video on Windowing Fusible Appliqué at **FonsandPorter. com/Window**

Quilt Assembly

1. Lay out blocks as shown in Quilt Top Assembly Diagram.

2. Join blocks into rows; join rows to complete quilt center.

Finishing

1. Divide backing into 2 (2½-yard [2.3m]) lengths. Cut 1 piece in half lengthwise to make 2 narrow panels. Join 1 narrow panel to each side of wider panel; press seam allowances toward narrow panels.

2. Layer backing, batting, and quilt top; baste. Quilt as desired. Quilt shown was quilted with various echoing curves in Petals, parallel lines in white squares, leaf vein motif in orange shapes, and 1" (3cm) squares in each block's corners (Quilting Diagram).

3. Join 2¼" (6cm)-wide turquoise strips into 1 continuous piece for straight-grain French-fold binding. Add binding to quilt.

Designer Profile

Jenifer Dick began quilting in 1993 when she signed up for a beginning quiltmaking class. In 2001, she discovered appliqué and it changed her life. Jenifer has authored four books on topics from traditional to modern quiltmaking and frequently speaks about and teaches appliqué techniques. In December, look for her new book, *Modern Appliqué Workbook*. Jenifer lives in Harrisonville, Missouri, with her husband and three children. Follow her on her blog at 42quilts.com.

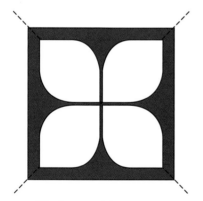

Block Assembly Diagram

Make 10

Make 9

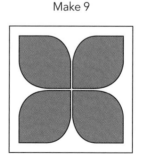

Make 1

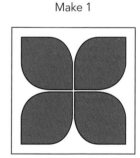

Block Diagrams

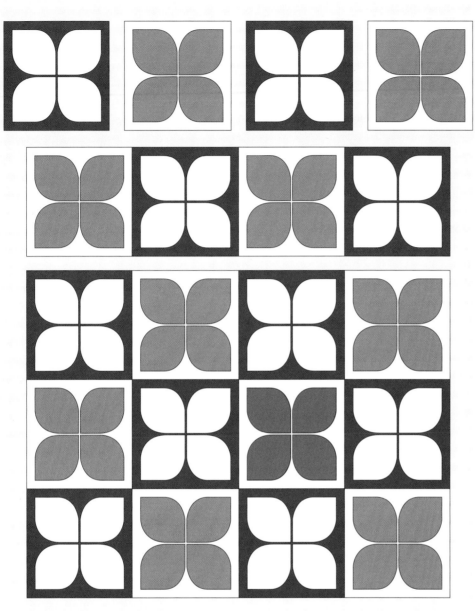

Quilt Top Assembly Diagram

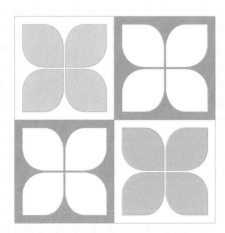

Doodle your own quilting design here.

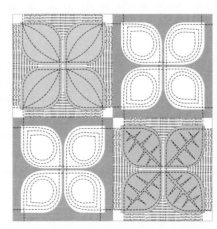

Quilting Diagram

Adding a Hanging Sleeve

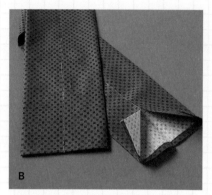

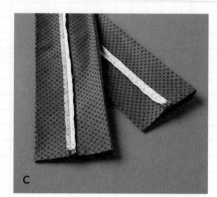

If you'd like to hang up your quilt—in your home or at a quilt show, perhaps—you'll need a hanging sleeve on the back. Follow these steps to make a standard-size, durable sleeve for any quilt.

1. Cut and piece together 8½" (22cm)-wide straight-grain fabric strips to make a strip the exact width of finished quilt. Fold the ends in twice (¼" [6mm] and ¼" [6mm] again). Topstitch close to folds to finish each end of the sleeve (Photo A).

2. Fold the sleeve in half lengthwise and press to mark center. With wrong sides facing, press the long sides of the sleeve so they meet in the center; press. The fold lines provide the guide needed for attaching sleeve to quilt (Photo B).

3. Fold sleeve in half wrong sides together; stitch ¼" (6mm) seam. Carefully press seam allowance open, maintaining previous fold lines (Photo C).

4. Center the sleeve across the width on back of quilt. The edge of the sleeve should lie just inside binding on each side of quilt. Using one

lengthwise fold as a guide, pin top of sleeve in place ½" (13mm) to ¾" (19mm) from the top edge. Pin along bottom fold line (Photo D). Blindstitch sleeve to back of quilt.

The sleeve will fit flat against the quilt from fold line to fold line; the rest of the sleeve will cup out, giving the sleeve space to fit around the hanging rod without distorting the quilt.

Tips

- It is not necessary to make a 4" (10cm)-wide sleeve for small and miniature quilts. Usually we cut the sleeve for these quilts 3" (8cm) - to 4" (10cm) wide.
- If entering quilt in a show, check show rules for hanging sleeve requirements.
- If you are adding a sleeve before a quilt is bound, follow Step 1 to make clean-finished ends. With wrong sides together, fold the sleeve in half lengthwise; press. Baste sleeve to the top outside edge on back of quilt, aligning raw edges. Add binding to quilt stitching through all layers. Blindstitch the bottom of sleeve to quilt back ½" (13mm) away from fold on the part of the sleeve that will lie flat against the quilt.

The Future of Quilting Is Bright

Quilts aren't going anywhere.

As long as we are made of flesh and blood, as long as we have babies, get married, grieve the death of loved ones; as long as we want to craft a symbol of our love, our time, and our compassion to those who need it, we will make quilts.

But times have changed. How we learn and when we learn the quiltmaking process is wildly different from how people learned even one generation ago. We—you, me, the quilters who exist and those who haven't been born, yet—have a responsibility to all those quilts yet to be made in the name of love. There is no time for lamentation about "the good old days." There is only time to get busy learning, teaching, and sharing the love of quiltmaking to anyone and absolutely everyone who wants to know, no matter how old they are, how young they are, or whether they've ever lain eyes on a bobbin.

The future of quilting is bright. We hold the thread, the fabric, and the light.

(Spooly wrote that last part.)

Farmer's Market Tote

Flowers, baked goods, cherries, spinach? Bring it.

MATERIALS

⅝ yard (57cm) red stripe oilcloth (or laminated fabric)

⅝ yard (57cm) green print (or laminated fabric)

1¼ yards (1.1m) pre-made black bias tape

2 (24" [61cm]-long) pieces of 1"(5cm)-wide black nylon strapping

CUTTING

Measurements include ½" (13mm) seam allowances.

From red stripe oilcloth, cut:
- 1 (8" [20cm]-wide) strip. From strip, cut 2 (8" × 15" [20cm × 38cm]) C rectangles and 1 (8" × 13" [20cm × 33cm]) D rectangle.
- 1 (13" [33cm]-wide) strip. From strip, cut 2 (13" × 15" [33cm × 38cm]) B rectangles and 1 (6½" [17cm]) A square.

From green print oilcloth, cut:
- 1 (8" [30cm]-wide) strip. From strip, cut 2 (8" × 15" [20cm × 38cm]) C rectangles and 1 (8" ×13" [20cm × 33cm]) D rectangle.
- 1 (13" [33cm]-wide) strip. From strip, cut 2 (13" × 15" [30cm × 38cm]) B rectangles.

Fabric Note
Lisa used oilcloth from Oilcloth by the Yard.

Editor's Note: We run a small project in each issue of Quilty. People like them. It can be fun to do a small sewing or quilting project in between larger ones, or just for the fun of it. This totebag is something that many of us would pay top dollar for at a cute boutique. It's so cool that if you can sew, you can make one yourself—at less cost to you and totally made-to-order.

PROJECT BY Lisa Stone
12" × 14" × 7" (30cm × 36cm × 18cm)
Beginner Level 2

Bag Assembly

1. Fold under ¼" (6mm) on all outer edges of red stripe A square. Topstitch close to top edge.

2. Referring to Bag Front Diagram, center pocket on 1 green print B rectangle, with top edge of pocket 4" (10cm) from top edge of B rectangle; keep in place using tape. Stitch pocket to B rectangle along sides and bottom edge of pocket. Reinforce stitching at top corners of pocket.

3. Mark corners of each D rectangle ½" (13mm) in on each corner. Mark B and C rectangles ½" (13mm) from each bottom corner.

4. Join 2 red stripe C rectangles and 2 green print B rectangles to form a tube. Start at marks and sew from bottom to top of bag, leaving bottom seam allowance free (Bag Assembly Diagram).

5. Join 1 D rectangle to front/sides/back tube, matching marks at corners. Start and stop stitching at corner marks.

6. Repeat steps 3–5 using remaining B, C, and D rectangles to make bag lining.

7. Turn bag with the pocket right side out; smooth out corners.

8. Place lining inside bag with pocket, aligning seams.

9. Fold bias tape over both top edges and stitch to enclose top edge of bag.

10. Tape 1 strap to front of bag, placing strap 2" (5cm) from side seams as shown in Strap Diagrams. Check to be sure strap is not twisted. Stitch across strap ends. Fold strap up and topstitch to reinforce.

11. Repeat for strap on back of bag.

Designer Profile

Lisa Stone has been quilting for over twenty-five years. She has been married for almost thirty years! Three children and five grandchildren. Her bags are reversible and can be wiped out! Also good for wet bathing suits and towels.

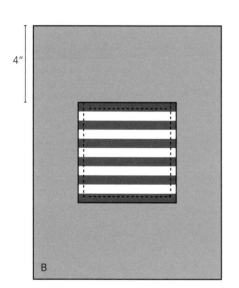

Bag Front Diagram

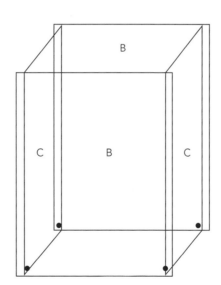

Bag Assembly Diagram

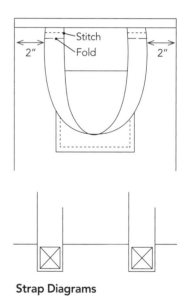

Strap Diagrams

Tip Top Tips

- When sewing oilcloth, use a long stitch length, ⅛" (3mm) or longer. Shorter stitch lengths create too many holes and can weaken the seams. Stitch slowly as you gently guide fabric through sewing machine.
- Use tape to hold pocket to bag front before stitching. Pins leave permanent holes in the material. Remove tape just before sewing that section.
- Because pins leave permanent holes in the material, use pins only within seam allowances. Or, use binding and hem clips, large paper clips, or binder clips to hold pieces together.

Video!
Try a bunch of new blocks! *Quilty's* "Blocks-a-Go-Go" episodes show you how. Try this: **HeyQuilty.com/Shoo.**

Gift Card Pockets

MATERIALS

3 (5" × 7" [13cm × 18cm]) rectangles assorted gray prints

3 (4" × 7" [10cm × 18cm]) rectangles assorted solids and prints

3 (5" × 7" [13cm × 18cm]) rectangles woven fusible interfacing

Assorted fabric scraps for embellishing

¼ yard (23cm) paper-backed fusible web

CUTTING

Measurements include ¼" (6mm) seam allowances.

From (4" × 7" [10cm × 18cm]) rectangles assorted solids and prints, cut each:
- 2 (3¼" × 3¾" [8cm × 10cm]) B rectangles.

From ¼ yard (23cm) paper-backed fusible web, cut:
- 6 (¼" × 2" [6mm × 51mm]) rectangles. Fuse assorted fabric scraps to remainder. Plan, then cut a variety of circles, squares, and rectangles for embellishment of finished B rectangles.

 Fabric Note
Fabrics are from Emily's stash.

(Don't) show 'em the money.

Editor's Note: Our friend Emily likes to work in miniature, and these little gift card pockets are a great way to "try tiny" yourself. In an age where a lot of gift-giving is in 0's and 1's, we thought putting fabric around plastic was a very *Quilty* idea. These go together fast and are fun to do in a group, too.

QUILT BY Emily Lang
2¾" × 4¼" (7cm × 11cm)
Beginner Level 1

Gift Card Pocket Assembly

1. Fuse 1 (5" × 7" [13cm × 18cm]) gray print rectangle to 1 (5" × 7" [13cm × 18cm]) woven fusible interfacing rectangle to make 1 unit (Fuse Diagrams). Cut unit into 2 (3¼" × 4¾" [10cm × 12cm]) A rectangles. Make 3 sets of 2, total.

2. Join 1 set of fused A rectangles with right sides facing. Stitch around outer edges with ¼" (6mm) seam allowance, leaving 2" (5cm) opening for turning, as shown in Unit Assembly Diagrams. Trim corners and press ¼" (6mm) seam flaps at opening toward unit. Apply 1 (¼" × 2" [6mm × 51mm]) strip of paper-backed fusible web and press to a ¼" (6mm) flap. Turn right side out through opening, then fuse opening by pressing unit flat. Make 3 Unit A.

3. In same manner, join 2 matching B rectangles (Unit Assembly Diagrams). Make 3 Unit B. Arrange prepared circles, squares, and rectangles to embellish B units. Press to fuse in place.

Finishing

1. Place B unit on top of A unit, meeting edges at one end. Stitch ⅛" (3mm) seam completely around outer edges (Gift Card Pockets Assembly Diagrams). Make 3 assorted.

We step this out on our show at **HeyQuilty.com/GiftCard.**

Designer Profile

Emily Lang is a wife, mother, and part-time bookseller. She has a love affair with shrinking complex quilt blocks down to teeny-tiny sizes and can't get enough of the bold saturated colors found in modern fabrics. To learn more about Emily, check out her blog at mommysnaptime.blogspot.com.

Interfacing

Make 1 set of 3

A

A

Fuse Diagrams

2" (5cm)   ¼" (6mm)   Press / Trim   ¼" × 2" (6mm × 51mm) Fusible Strip

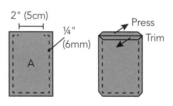
A

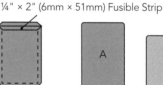
A   B

Unit Assembly Diagrams

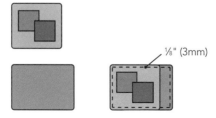

⅛" (3mm)

Gift Card Pockets Assembly Diagrams

Sheyenne Manning & Diane Tomlinson

Sheyenne Manning serves as Online Editor at Fons & Porter.

What do you do to make *Quilty*?
I'm the Interactive Editor on Team Quilty, and I have three major jobs: I write the meta information for each quilt project that goes on the web so the projects are more easily found by search engines; before the magazine goes to newsstands, I make sure all the links work; and I make sure all the videos that are linked from the magazine are posted to QNNtv.com before customers see the magazine.

I heard you get weird looks at the office. How come?
I have to watch the videos so I can write up descriptions and meta information; when I'm watching the videos with my headphones in, I frequently burst into random, gratuitous laughter. My co-workers assume I'm watching *Quilty* if they hear spontaneous laughter from my cubicle.

What makes *Quilty* great?
I've watched a lot of quilting videos during my time in the quilting industry and I'm never so entertained as when I'm watching *Quilty*. It's like when they let you watch *Bill Nye The Science Guy* as a kid and you're happy because it doesn't feel like school. Second, *Quilty* answers questions we're all afraid to ask, like "Why does my bobbin do that?" Let's face it, not all of us grew up with a mother or grandmother who taught us everything we know about quilting and we have questions! *Quilty*'s got you covered.

Diane Tomlinson, in addition to being an expert quilter and teacher, is Assistant Editor of *Quilty* and a number of other Fons & Porter titles, including *Love of Quilting* and *Easy Quilts.*

What makes *Quilty* different from other quilting magazines?
I think it's our basic and unique approach to quilting and design. It gives ownership to the quilter in her/his designs and projects, whatever their skill level.

What's your advice to someone who wants to submit a quilt to any magazine, not just *Quilty*?
Make sure it's your best! Make sure it's your exclusive design, too. And give inclusive information about your quilt. Include size, fabric choices, how you will finish your quilt with quilting, and a completion date helps, too.

Sheyenne, obviously the most fabulous Online Editor at Fons & Porter (or anywhere else).

Diane Tomlinson, master quilter, professional quilt wrangler, and general *Quilty* gatekeeper.

You wear so many hats for Team Quilty: editor, quilter, photography stylist, etc. We should call you "The Glue" for all you do to hold everything together. What's your favorite part of the job?
The people! I love meeting new people and get inspired every day by their designs—and how excited they are when their designs are accepted. It's contagious!

Preparing for Machine Quilting

1. Find the crosswise center of the backing fabric by folding it in half. Mark the middle with a pin on each side. Lay backing down on a table or floor, right side down. Tape corners and edges of backing to your surface with masking or painter's tape so that the backing is taut but not pulled so tight it wrinkles or buckles (Photo A).

2. Create a "quilt sandwich" by layering your backing, batting, and quilt top. Put the batting down on the backing (Photos B and C).

3. Now lay down your top, after marking the crosswise center just like you did with the backing (Photos D and E).

4. Baste your quilt with safety pins. Basting means to hold loosely together. Do about a fist-width's distance between your pins and make sure you're taking a "bite" of all the layers and smoothing from the center out as you go (Photo F). See Basting Three Ways for other basting methods.

Watch This Episode!
HeyQuilty.com/Basting

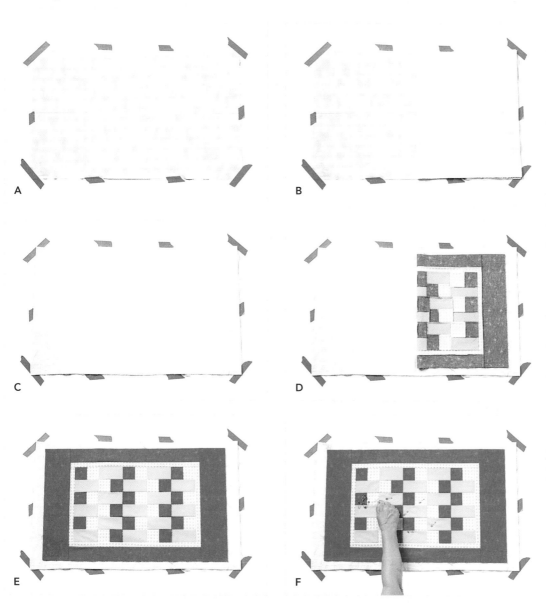

Stitch in the Ditch Machine Quilting

For some novice quilters, it's a relief to just "stitch in the ditch," instead of creating a quilting pattern. To "SITD" means to quilt in the seams of your patchwork.

1. Prepare your quilt for machine quilting. (See Preparing for Machine Quilting on previous page.)

2. Attach your walking foot to your machine. Consult your sewing machine owner's manual if you need help with this. Note: Not all machines come standard with a walking foot. If you're planning to quilt your quilt, make sure you've got a walking foot before the big day arrives (Photo A).

3. Take a look at your quilt. If it has a lot of piecing, you may not want to quilt every "ditch." Perhaps quilt around the perimeter of each block and find an "X" or a "T" within the block to follow. You want to quilt a continuous line with as little stopping and starting as possible, so map out your plan before you begin. A chalk fabric pencil that will brush off can help you see where you're going (Photo B).

4. Work carefully—and not too fast. Quilt directly in the ditches you've chosen. It's smart to set your machine so that the needle stops in the down position. This holds your place when you get to a point where you turn to go in a different direction (Photo C).

5. The last step is to run a stitch a scant ⅛" (3mm) around the perimeter of the quilt. This helps keep your edges nice and neat before you bind.

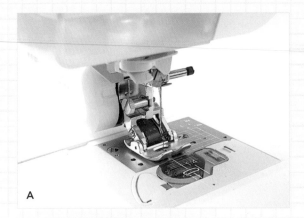

A

Watch a Quilty video to learn how to SITD!
HeyQuilty.com/SITD.

B

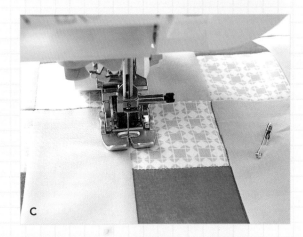

C

Spooly Says

"Make a sample quilt sandwich and practice a little before you tackle your quilt. You'll learn a lot!"

Basting Three Ways

1. Refer to Preparing for Machine Quilting to properly prepare your quilt sandwich. Once you have a smooth, bubble-free sandwich, you're ready to baste.

2. To baste with pins—advised when machine quilting at home—set a pile of curved basting pins nearby. Place pins about a fist-width's distance apart, approx. 2½" (6cm). Use a pin-closing tool or a grapefruit spoon to help you close your pins, especially if you're basting a large quilt (Photo A).

3. To hand baste, thread a curved basting needle (or any needle you're comfortable with) with a contrasting thread color. Continuously and loosely stitch through all layers of your sandwich (Photo B).

4. If using basting spray, you'll baste as you make your sandwich, not after. Work in halves. Once the backing is taped down, place your batting and then fold back one half. Spray the underside with basting spray. Lay batting back down. Repeat with other side, smoothing out your two layers (Photos C and D). Now repeat that process with the top of your quilt—and get quilting, friend (Photo E)!

Interested in a video on basting? Check it out at **HeyQuilty.com/Basting**.

A

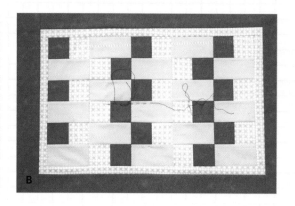

B

C

D

E

Tying a Quilt

When is a finished quilt not exactly a quilt but really close? When you tie it.

Tie your quilt with strong cotton, synthetic, or worsted weight yarn, pearl cotton, or embroidery floss. Whatever you use, make sure it's thin enough to pull through your fabric without making a big hole, but thick enough to secure your layers.

You'll need your scissors and a darning or tapestry needle. There are curved needles that are great for this method, too. Space your ties evenly, no more than 4" (10cm) apart, otherwise stuff's going to shift and be sad. Tying at the corners and centers of blocks is recommended provided your blocks aren't enormous.

Configure your quilt sandwich and baste with safety pins. Now you're ready to go. Here is a popular method for successfully tying a quilt—er, comforter—for maximum enjoyment and durability.

Ties on the Front

1. Thread your needle with a long length of yarn. Don't knot the end. Take a small stitch from the top through all three layers. Pull up the yarn and leave a 3"–4" (8cm–10cm) tail. Don't snip anything yet.

2. Move to the next place you want to tie. Take another small stitch through all layers, leaving long, loose lengths of yarn between tie positions on your quilt top. This will eventually be cut and become the tails that you tie off! Nifty. Be generous, therefore, with the amount of yarn you leave between your stitches (Photo A).

3. Place all your ties.

4. Cut each length of yarn midway between stitches. Wrap right yarn tail around the left tail, forming a half-square knot. Tie it tight (Photo B).

A

B

Video!
For a great video tutorial, check this out! **HeyQuilty.com/Tying**

Tip

Remember, there are usually several methods for every quilting objective. . . find the technique that works for you! Want ties on the back? Visit HeyQuilty. com for an alternate version.

Binding 101

Learn binding!
HeyQuilty.com/Binding

We like this method for attaching binding to the edge of a quilt. Observe other quilters, ask questions, watch videos, and in no time, binding will be no biggie.

Preparing Binding

Strips for quilt binding may be cut either on the straight of grain or on the bias. For this demo, cut strips on the straight of grain.

1. Measure the perimeter of your quilt and add approximately 24" (61cm) to allow for mitered corners and finished ends.

2. Cut the necessary number of strips to achieve desired length. We like to cut binding strips 2¼" (57mm) wide, but some like 2½" (64mm). It's your choice.

3. Join your strips into 1 continuous piece using diagonal seams (Photo A). Press the seams open.

4. Press your binding in half lengthwise, wrong sides facing, to make French-fold binding (Photo B).

Attaching Binding

Attach the binding to your quilt using a walking foot. (This prevents puckering when sewing through the five layers.)

    Choose starting point along one side of the quilt. Do not start at a corner. Match the two raw edges of the binding strip to the raw edge of the quilt top. Stitch. The pressed binding edge will be free and to left of seam line (Photo C). Leave a 12" (30cm) or longer tail of binding strip dangling from beginning point.

A

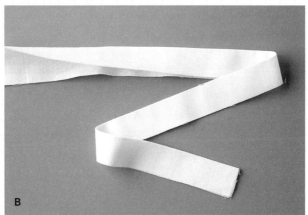

B

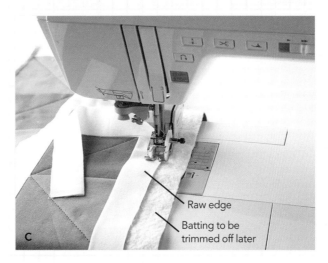

C

Raw edge

Batting to be trimmed off later

Spooly Says

"According to a 2010 survey, 73% of quilters are online. The Internet is a great tool for inspiration, instruction, and community." (Quilting In America Survey, 2010–Creative Crafts Group)

Mitered Corners

1. Place a pin ¼" (6mm) from corner to mark where you will stop stitching. Stop stitching ¼" (6mm) from corner; backstitch, and remove quilt from sewing machine. Rotate quilt quarter turn and fold binding straight up, away from corner, forming 45-degree-angle fold (Photo D). Bring binding straight down in line with next edge to be sewn, leaving top fold even with raw edge of previously sewn side (Photo E). Begin stitching at top edge, sewing through all layers.

2. Stop stitching about 8" (20cm) away from starting point, leaving about a 12" (30cm) tail at end. Bring beginning and end of binding to center of 8" (20cm) opening and fold each back, leaving about ¼" (6mm) space between the two folds of binding (Photo F). Finger press the folds. Allowing this ¼" (6mm) extra space is critical, as binding tends to stretch when it is stitched to the quilt. If the folded ends meet at this point, your binding will be too long for the space after the ends are joined.

3. Open binding and draw line across wrong side of binding on fold line, as shown in Photo G. Draw line along lengthwise fold of binding at same spot to create an X (Photo H).

4. With edge of ruler at marked X, line up 45-degree angle marking on ruler with one long side of binding. Draw diagonal line across binding as shown in Photo I. Repeat for other end of binding. Lines must angle in same direction (Photo J).

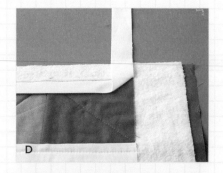

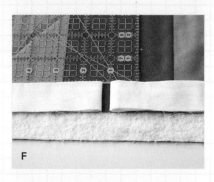

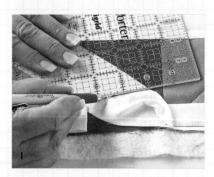

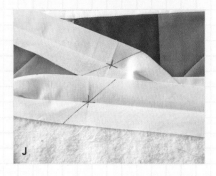

Hungry for more video on binding? Check out Liz Porter's famous technique at **DailyCraftTV.com/Binding.**

5. Pin binding ends together with right sides facing, pin-matching diagonal lines as shown in Photo K. Binding ends will be at right angles to each other. Machine-stitch along diagonal line, removing pins as you stitch.

6. Lay binding against quilt to double check that it is correct length (Photo L). Trim ends of binding ¼" (6mm) from diagonal seam.

7. Finger press diagonal seam open (Photo M). Fold binding in half and finish stitching the binding to your quilt (Photo N).

Hand Stitching Binding to Quilt Back

1. Trim any excess batting and quilt back with scissors or a rotary cutter (Photo O). Leave enough batting (about ⅛" [3mm] beyond quilt top) to fill binding uniformly when it is turned to quilt back.

2. Bring pressed edge of binding to quilt back so that it covers machine stitching. Blindstitch folded edge to quilt backing, using a few pins just ahead of stitching to hold binding in place (Photo P).

3. Continue stitching to corner. Fold under unstitched binding from next side, forming a 45-degree angle and a mitered corner. Stitch mitered folds on both front and back (Photo Q). Good job.

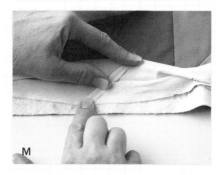

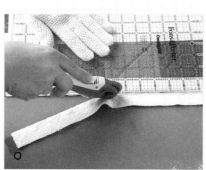

Project Templates

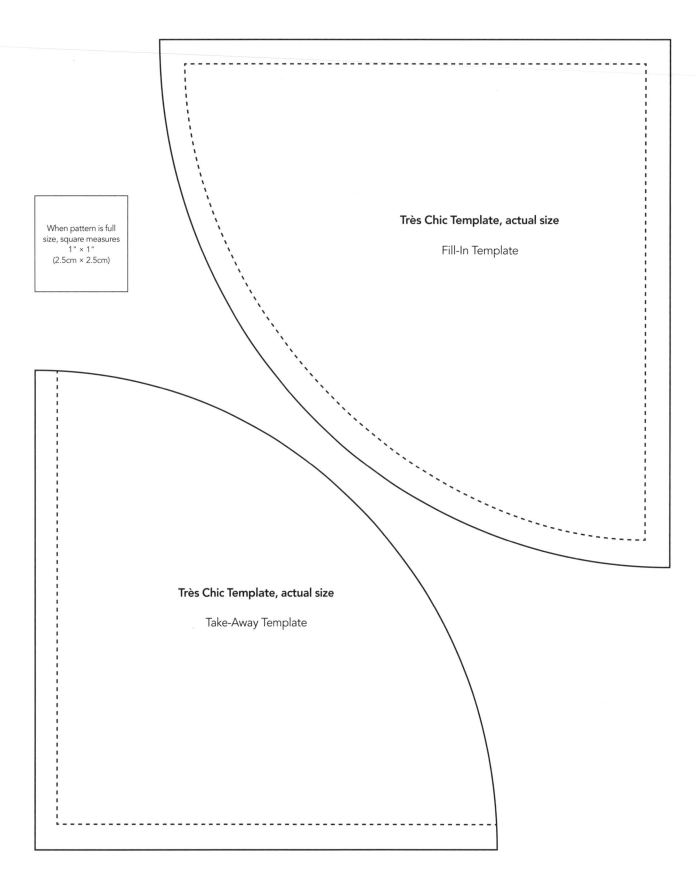

When pattern is full size, square measures 1" × 1" (2.5cm × 2.5cm)

Très Chic Template, actual size

Fill-In Template

Très Chic Template, actual size

Take-Away Template

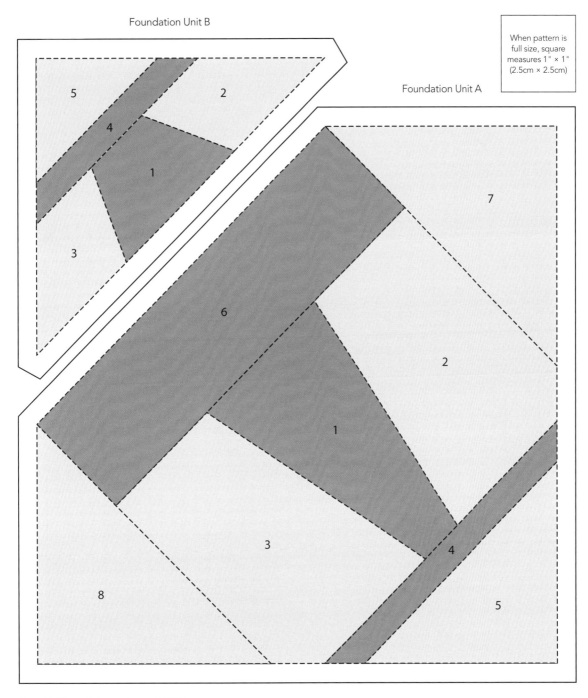

Foundation Unit B

Foundation Unit A

When pattern is
full size, square
measures 1" × 1"
(2.5cm × 2.5cm)

Amelia Template, enlarge 125%

Wheeee!

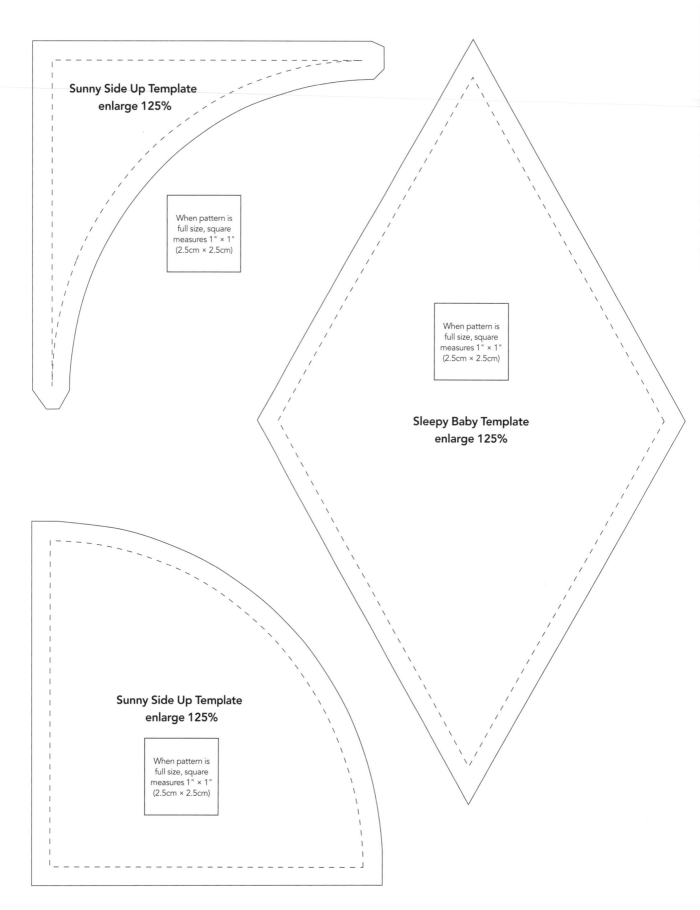

Sunny Side Up Template
enlarge 125%

When pattern is
full size, square
measures 1" × 1"
(2.5cm × 2.5cm)

When pattern is
full size, square
measures 1" × 1"
(2.5cm × 2.5cm)

Sleepy Baby Template
enlarge 125%

Sunny Side Up Template
enlarge 125%

When pattern is
full size, square
measures 1" × 1"
(2.5cm × 2.5cm)

When pattern is full size, square measures 1" × 1" (2.5cm × 2.5cm)

Petal, actual size

Pattern shown full size for use with fusible web. Add ³⁄₁₆" (5mm) seam allowance for hand appliqué.

Mod Shape Template

"Psst... Hi."

Index

Dedication

This book is dedicated to all the first quilts
and the quilters who make them.

Acknowledgments

Many people make *Quilty*. Their presence in this book is
hopefully the firmest acknowledgement of their hard work,
but in case it's not clear: Thank you, Team Quilty. From
technical writing to sound editing, from url redirects to
customer service folks who put in DVD orders, thank you.

To the *Quilty* sponsors past, present, and future, there is no
show without you. Thank you for finding room for the
beginner. They'll always love you for it—and so will we.

Thank you to Marianne Fons for lending priceless credibility
and for helping with absolutely everything.
You're the best guest, by the way.

And thank you, *Quilty* fan, for trying something new.

Metric Conversion Chart

To convert	to	multiply by
Inches	Centimeters	2.54
Centimeters	Inches	0.4
Feet	Centimeters	30.5
Centimeters	Feet	0.03
Yards	Meters	0.9
Meters	Yards	1.1

   www.fwcommunity.com

19   18   17   16   15   5   4   3   2   1

Distributed in Canada by Fraser Direct
100 Armstrong Avenue
Georgetown, ON, Canada L7G 5S4
Tel: (905) 877-4411

Distributed in the U.K. and Europe by F&W MEDIA INTERNATIONAL
Brunel House, Newton Abbot, Devon, TQ12 4PU, England
Tel: (+44) 1626 323200, Fax: (+44) 1626 323319
Email: enquiries@fwmedia.com

Distributed in Australia by Capricorn Link
P.O. Box 704, S. Windsor NSW, 2756 Australia
Tel: (02) 4560 1600, Fax: (02) 4577 5288
E-mail: books@capricornlink.com.au

SRN: T4985
ISBN-13: 978-1-4402-4318-9

Edited by Team Quilty
Designed by Clare Finney
Production coordinated by Jennifer Bass
Photography by Team Quilty

About the Author

Writer, teacher, and designer Mary Fons was born in Iowa, is based in Chicago, and is usually out on the road. Mary co-hosts the nationally-airing PBS program Fons & Porter's *Love of Quilting* along with her mom, beloved quilter and educator Marianne Fons. In 2010, Mary successfully pitched *Quilty*, the online show offered weekly on QNNtv.com. Targeted primarily to the beginner quilter, *Quilty* offers instruction, guidance, and inspiration to those who want to learn to make a quilt, whatever their age or experience level. In 2012, Mary became editor of *Quilty* magazine. Mary believes that being a quilter means being a part of the coolest legacy in American history. For more about Mary, visit MaryFons.com.

So many quilts, so little time.

Quilty magazine

If you've haven't already signed up to get *Quilty* regularly, what are you waiting for?! Sign up for our autoship option to get all the latest designs and tips mailed straight to your door every other month. Or get a digital subscription for prompt inbox delivery. Visit www.heyquilty.com for all the details.

50 Quilts from Quiltmaker

Favorite Blocks from the 100 Blocks Series from the editors of *Quiltmaker* magazine

For the first time, the editors of *Quiltmaker* have compiled their 50 favorite quilts from the popular 100 Blocks Series in one place. Each technique-based chapter features quilts (sizes ranging from small projects to bed quilt) including: appliqué, mixed techniques, patchwork piecing, foundation piecing and creative borders, with an appendix of techniques.

502 Quilting Motifs

Designs for Hand or Machine Quilting from the editors of *Quiltmaker* magazine

Quiltmaker magazine has been publishing quilting designs for your patchwork quilt for a generation; collected here are another 502 beloved designs that can be adapted to fit your quilt.

Fons&Porter

These and other fine Fons & Porter titles are available at your local craft retailer, bookstore or online supplier, or visit our website at www.shopfonsandporter.com.